OREN

OREN

A Personal Collection of Recipes
and Stories From Tel Aviv

ODED OREN

Hardie Grant

BOOKS

INTRODUCTION

My love for food started at an early age; I grew up in Tel Aviv, Israel, in an Ashkenazi Jewish family. Ashkenazi Jews are from Central and Eastern Europe, and the food culture is fascinating, with many incredible dishes, but as I got older and experienced the many different food cultures that exist in Tel Aviv, I found myself more drawn to other styles of cooking. Through friends and family, I was introduced to Iraqi, Moroccan, Tunisian and Libyan dishes that have continued to influence the food I create today. As well as this home cooking, I used to love going out to eat. Visiting different restaurants with my dad was a big part of my childhood; sometimes we would go to Kerem HaTeimanim, a district where you can get traditional homestyle Yemenite food – a lot of which was cooked in huge pots over a kerosene light, which is essentially a candle, overnight. The smell was insane – so fragrant and intense; huge pots of rich bone broth filled with offal, grains and beans. Other times we would go to a famous steakhouse called Mi va Mi and sit at the counter in front of an open charcoal grill. They served chopped salad made in front of you, drizzled with copious amounts of tahini, and grilled pork neck stuffed into warm pita.

After I finished my education at the age of eighteen, I had the opportunity for some headspace to think about what I wanted to do next. I quite quickly realised that I wanted to cook for a living. I attended the Tadmor culinary school, which was the only cookery school in Israel back then. At the time, the style of food that was popular in restaurants was very different to the kind of food I cook today; there was a lot of classic French and European cooking. Although my time at the school gave me the fundamentals of cooking and taught me the essential elements of working in a professional kitchen, this style of food didn't speak to me in the same way as the Mediterranean and Middle Eastern foods I'd loved as a kid. I started working in kitchens immediately, working in a small restaurant in Paris for a year. It was a demanding job of gruelling fifteen-hour days. Although it was an incredible experience to find myself fully immersed in a real French restaurant kitchen, in the end I decided to return to Israel.

I worked in various restaurants in Tel Aviv, gaining experience and learning all the time. It didn't matter to me which kitchen I was in, or which restaurant – I wanted to absorb all of the knowledge and skill around me, picking up new techniques and discovering how I liked to cook as I went along. It was the food that mattered – as always, it was my safe place, and there was something therapeutic about just focusing on the food, wherever I was.

When I was about twenty-six, I started working at Turkiz, a renowned restaurant in Tel Aviv. I began as a line cook, then graduated to a sous-chef position, and after about eighteen months I became head chef. I was very young, and it was a big responsibility: the restaurant was well-known, and I was in charge of a big kitchen serving 200 covers. This was when I properly started to explore and develop my own style. It wasn't easy, but I relished the challenge and worked very hard. Eventually, though, I knew I needed to make a big change. So, in 2011, after eight years at Turkiz, I decided to move to the UK.

I started working in a couple of restaurants to get a feel for the food scene. I needed a break from the intensity of a professional kitchen, so decided to take on private cheffing work and consultancy for a while, but ultimately I missed the energy of a restaurant. I began doing a few pop-ups, cooking in cafés and other small venues – and then something clicked. This wasn't about money or recognition: it was about connecting to the dishes that had first captured my imagination as a child and being able to share the experience with others. I realised that opening my own place was the way to do it – it would give me the chance to connect, build a community and see people eating my food. I kept on with the pop-up gigs, and then I was invited to be a guest chef at a place called Louie Louie in Camberwell, South London. For six months, I travelled there every day from east London. We got a fantastic review in the *Guardian* from food critic Jay Rayner, and that was a huge boost; it's unusual for a pop-up to get this kind of national press attention, so I knew I was on the right track.

The food that has always spoken to me, and the food that I cook today, is simple, bold, ingredients-focused and fresh. It's the food from my home; the food that I grew up with. I'd never thought it would be 'special' enough to serve in a restaurant, but my mentality was evolving. I wasn't a young chef trying to prove something and cook complex, fancy dishes: I just wanted to make real, genuine and tasty food; to return to the basics – but do it better.

I opened Oren in 2019 – which was possibly the worst timing in restaurant history, as we had about four or five months of trade before the first COVID lockdown. But, in that brief time, we had a great response: the restaurant filled up, and the feedback was great. It was a very difficult period, but the positive I've taken from it was that we were able to really connect to the community around us. And, as it always has been for me, food once again became a place of safety and comfort, and we were able to offer others the reassurance and joy of delicious food during such an uncertain and challenging time. In a way, the pandemic made the restaurant what it is today – a place for sharing and connection.

The dishes in this book are friendly, easy and accessible – Hake Arayes with Lamb Fat and Spiced Yoghurt (page 201), Lamb and Beef Mince Kebabs with Burnt Aubergine (page 218) and Warm Freekeh Salad with Laben Kishk with Pine Nuts (page 186), to name a few – and there are no intimidating techniques or hard-to-find ingredients.

That's really the joy of food, for me, and now I want to share some of these recipes with you. The dishes in this book are friendly, easy and accessible – there are no intimidating techniques or hard-to-find ingredients. Some of them have been on the menu at the restaurant or at my pop-ups for years; some of them are dishes I cook at home for family and friends; some of them featured on the takeaway menus we developed during lockdown. The most important thing – and I'll say it again and again throughout the book – is to always try and source the best possible fresh produce you can. This style of cooking is all about the ingredients, so you need to start with the best: fresh, in season and full of flavour.

I hope these recipes will inspire you, and that you too will find a way to connect with others through sharing the joy of simple, fresh, delicious food.

CHAPTER 1

SMALL PLATES

The recipes in this chapter are things that stay on the table for the duration of a meal. They are almost like condiments – they can be eaten with bread, or used to enhance the flavours of other dishes; burnt chilli harissa is amazing smeared on warm pita then piled with lamb and beef kebabs and a dollop of tahini.

You can make all of these dishes in advance and keep them in the refrigerator for a few days, so they can last across several meals and be at the ready to make your table feel that bit more abundant.

LABNEH

Makes 1.3 kg (2 lb 4 oz lb)

2.6 kg (5 lb 7 oz) Greek
    yoghurt
25 g (1 oz) fine sea salt
1 tablespoon lemon juice
za'atar, to garnish
olive oil, to garnish
pine nuts (optional),
    to garnish

Labneh goes with everything: I like to serve it with olive oil and za'atar, and it's also fantastic served with blinis instead of crème fraîche for a lighter, tangier finish. If you wish, you can opt to use sheep or goat's milk yoghurt if you like a bit more tang than your average cow's milk yoghurt.

Whisk the ingredients in a bowl then transfer into a muslin cloth. Grab the edges of the cloth and make a knot at the top. Hang the muslin over the kitchen sink and leave to strain for at least 24 hours, or up to 3 days if the temperature isn't too warm. After this time, half of the liquid should have drained away. Transfer to a sealed container and store in the refrigerator. It will keep for up to 1 week.

Serve with plenty of za'atar and olive oil. I like to also add some pine nuts as a garnish.

ZA'ATAR WITH OLIVE OIL

Makes about 250 g (9 oz)

55 g (2 oz) dried wild oregano
50 g (1¾ oz) sumac
165 g (5¾ oz) toasted white
   sesame seeds
2 teaspoons fine sea salt
2 tablespoons olive oil

This recipe is a great way to introduce za'atar into your kitchen. Try to get hold of mountain oregano, and use toasted sesame seeds, as that makes all the difference.

Mix all the ingredients together then store in an airtight container in a cool, dark place. The za'atar will keep for up to 2 months.

TZATZIKI

Makes 350 g (12½ oz)

100 g (3½ oz) cucumber,
    finely diced and squeezed
    from excess liquids
2 garlic cloves, crushed
juice of ½ lemon
250 g (9 oz) Labneh
    (page 16)
sea salt and freshly ground
    black pepper
extra-virgin olive oil,
    for drizzling

In this version of tzatziki, I use labneh rather than yoghurt, which results in a thicker consistency. I like it really garlicky, so if you're like me then feel free to add more than suggested.

Add the cucumber, garlic and lemon juice to the labneh in a bowl and mix well. Adjust the seasoning if necessary. Drizzle with olive oil.

OREN

HOUSE PICKLES

Makes 3 kg (6 lb 8 oz)

7 litres (1.85 gallons) water
350 g (12 oz) coarse sea salt
1.5 kg (3 lb 5 oz) cauliflower,
    separated into small
    florets
1 kg (2 lb 4 oz) carrots,
    peeled and cut into
    3 mm (1⁄16 in)-thick discs
1 large hispi cabbage,
    cut into thin wedges
    (stem intact)
8 celery stalks, cut into
    finger-sized chunks
100 g (3½ oz) mild red
    chillies, roughly chopped
100 g (3½ oz) garlic (whole
    cloves, unpeeled)
35 g (1¼ oz) allspice berries
5 bay leaves
150 g (5½ oz) dill

These pickles go with everything from salads and meat to wintery stews with beef and beans, and are a great way to cut through heavier flavours. This recipe is for proper fermented pickles, made using salt rather than vinegar. You'll need to taste them often to check when they're ready: you'll know they're ready because they will taste tangy rather than salty. The timing might vary depending on the climate and the temperature of your home – the process is slower in cold weather.

Mix 2 litres (68 fl oz/8½ cups) of the water with the salt in a large pan and bring to the boil, then remove from the heat and leave to cool. Once cool, mix it with the remaining 5 litres (175 fl oz/21½ cups) of water.

Mix all the vegetables, chillies, garlic, allspice berries and bay leaves together. Fill sterilised preserving jars with the vegetable mix. Top up with the brining liquid (prepared earlier) and cover with dill, making sure that everything is submerged in the liquid. Tightly close the lid and let the vegetables ferment at room temperature for 6–8 days. In the cooler months it will take 12–16 days. You'll know it's ready when the veggies go from tasting very salty to tasting pleasantly sour. Make sure you taste all the different vegetables, as some might be ready before the others. Once they're ready, transfer the jars to the refrigerator. They will keep for between 6–8 weeks.

LIBYAN QUICK PICKLES

**Makes 1 x 1.5 litre (51 fl oz)
Kilner (Mason) jar**

1 carrots, peeled and cut into
   julienne about 15 x 2 cm
   (16 x ¾ in)
1 cucumbers, cut into
   julienne about 15 x 2 cm
   (16 x ¾ in)
½ large kohlrabi, peeled
   and cut into julienne
   about 15 x 2 cm (16 x ¾ in)
½ fennel bulb, cut into
   julienne about 2.5 cm
   (1 in) wide
¼ cauliflower, separated into
   small florets
½ fresh green chilli,
   deseeded and cut into
   julienne about 15 x 2 cm
   (16 x ¾ in)
1 sweet red (bell) pepper,
   deseeded and cut into
   julienne about 15 x 2 cm
   (16 x ¾ in)
50 g (1¾ oz) radishes,
   cut into julienne about
   5 mm (¼ in) wide (if using
   small radishes, just cut
   in half)
1 garlic clove, bashed
125 ml (4 fl oz/½ cup) fresh
   lemon juice
1 tablespoon olive oil
2½ teaspoon sea salt

This Libyan pickle is halfway between a salad and long-fermented pickle. It works well paired with light dishes, such as Hummus (page 63) and Mejadra with Wild Rice, Speckled Lentils and Yoghurt Tahini (page 182).

Mix all the ingredients together, then place them in a clean 1.5 litre (51 fl oz) Kilner (Mason) jar. Add cold water (about 500 ml/17 fl oz) until all the vegetables are submerged. Tightly seal the jar and place in refrigerator.

The pickles are at their best after a couple of hours, and will last about 3 days in the refrigerator. Best eaten fresh on the day.

PICKLED CUCUMBERS

Makes 3 kg (6 lb 8 oz)

350 g (12 oz) coarse sea salt
7 litres (1.85 gallons) water
3 kg (6 lb 8 oz) cucumbers
100 g (3½ oz) mild red
    chillies, roughly chopped
100 g (3½ oz) garlic (whole
    cloves, unpeeled)
35 g (1¼ oz) allspice berries
5 bay leaves
150 g (5½ oz) dill

This is the kind of pickle that I used to eat as a child. It often features in Ashkenazi recipes, which serve traditional Central and Eastern European food, and it works really well with Cholent (page 184) and Chopped Liver Salad (page 232). I like the simplicity of this recipe as it draws upon the quality of the ingredients. It's best to use small cucumbers.

Mix 2 litres (68 fl oz/8½ cups) of the water with salt in a large pan and bring to the boil, then remove from the heat and leave to cool. Once cool, mix it with the remaining 5 litres (175 fl oz/21½ cups) of water.

Mix all the cucumbers, chillies, garlic, allspice berries and bay leaves together. Fill sterilised preserving jars with the vegetable mix. Top up with the brining liquid (prepared earlier) and cover with dill, making sure that everything is submerged in the liquid. Tightly close the lid and let the vegetables ferment at room temperature for 6–8 days. In the cooler months it will take 12–16 days. You'll know it's ready when the veggies go from tasting very salty to tasting pleasantly sour. Make sure you taste all the different vegetables, as some might be ready before the others. Once they're ready, transfer the jars to the refrigerator. They will keep for between 6–8 weeks.

PILPELCHUMA

Makes about 150 g (5½ oz)

10 g (¼ oz) sweet paprika
6 g (¼ oz) ground cumin
10 g (¼ oz) caraway seeds,
    ground
¼ teaspoon hot chilli powder
1 teaspoon fine sea salt
20 g (¾ oz) garlic cloves,
    finely chopped
75 ml (2½ fl oz) vegetable oil
25 ml (¾ fl oz) lemon juice

This Libyan condiment is based on the famous chraime (page 208). It's almost the Libyan equivalent of a Moroccan harissa, although caraway is the predominant flavour. I think it's delicious. You can serve it very simply with bread, or add it to any kind of stew – it would pair well with one featuring chickpeas (garbanzos) or beans. You could also rub it on fish and then grill for a spicy, fragrant finish. Experiment with what works for you.

Combine all the ingredients in a bowl then transfer to a clean jar and store in the refrigerator. It will keep for up to 1 week.

CHOPPED EGG SALAD WITH CARAMELISED ONIONS

Serves 2

3 large eggs
3 tablespoons vegetable oil
2 medium onions, finely diced
10 g (¼ oz) spring onions
    (scallions), finely sliced
1 teaspoon smooth
    Dijon mustard
pinch of freshly ground
    black pepper
35 g (1¼ oz) mayonnaise
2 g sea salt
1 tablespoon picked
    oregano leaves
squeeze of lemon juice
sea salt

This is a classic home-style dish in essence, though is a bit of an unusual version, because I have added caramelised onions for sweetness and mustard for a bit of a kick. The fresh oregano rounds it all out. Choose really good-quality free-range eggs – it makes a big difference to the end result.

Place the eggs in a small saucepan, cover with cold water, then bring to the boil and boil for 8–10 minutes. Remove the eggs from the heat and cool under cold running water. Make sure the eggs are cooled down thoroughly otherwise you won't be able to peel them easily.

Heat the vegetable oil in a frying pan (skillet) over a medium-high heat. Add the onions and fry for about 15 minutes, stirring occasionally, until dark brown and caramelised (but not burnt). Remove from the heat and leave to cool.

Peel the eggs and cut them into small dice or grate with a coarse cheese grater into a bowl. Add all the remaining ingredients, including the caramelised onions, and season with lemon juice and salt. The salad will keep in a sealed container in the refrigerator for up to 3 days.

FRIED AUBERGINE WITH SWEET RED PEPPERS AND CHILLI

Serves 6 as starters (appetisers)

2 aubergines (eggplant),
    cut into 2 cm (¾ in)-thick
    slices
sea salt
500 ml (17 fl oz) vegetable
    oil, for frying
100 ml (3½ fl oz/scant ½ cup)
    red wine vinegar
1 red (bell) pepper, deseeded
    and cut into 5 cm (2 in)
    batons
4 garlic cloves, thinly sliced
1 mild red chilli, thinly sliced
freshly ground black pepper
20 g (¾ oz) spring onions
    (scallions), finely sliced

This is a simple recipe, but it's important to take the time to follow it properly. First, don't skip the salting step: the extra effort is really worth it to draw out the excess liquid and get the best possible results. Next, make sure you take the time to fry the aubergines (eggplants) properly, working in small batches so you don't overcrowd the pan. Finally, remember to drain them of excess oil before combining them with the other ingredients. These small steps make such a difference to the final texture. This dish is best served at room temperature rather than piping hot, so let it sit for a little while and allow all those flavours to mingle.

Lay the slices of aubergine on a flat tray, spread out in a single layer. Sprinkle with some salt and leave for 20 minutes until the aubergine have released some of their liquid. Wipe off the excess liquid.

Heat the cooking oil in a deep pan over a medium-high heat until it reaches 180°C (360°F). Fry the aubergine slices in the oil, one small batch at the time (to avoid the oil cooling down too much) for about 3 minutes on each side (use tongs to flip them) until brown. Drain on paper towel.

Place the aubergines in a large mixing bowl. Pour over the vinegar and add the pepper, garlic and chilli. Season with salt and pepper, and mix well with your hands. Serve at room temperature with sliced spring onions sprinkled on top. The dish will keep in a sealed container in the refrigerator for up to 3 days.

BURNT CHILLI HARISSA
WITH GARLIC AND OLIVE OIL

Makes 300 g (10½ oz)

300 g (10½ oz) mild
   red chillies
3 garlic cloves, finely
   chopped
1 tablespoon olive oil
¼ teaspoon sea salt

This is my version of a traditional harissa, which is usually made with dried chillies ground to a paste with oil and garlic. We've been making it in the restaurant since we opened. There are no extra spices added – it's just charred fresh chillies, garlic and oil. It makes a great condiment that works with so many of the dishes in this book, adding a kick and a touch of smokiness that is really special.

Burn the chillies over an open flame (either on the hob or on a barbecue) for roughly 4–5 minutes, turning them until the skin has blackened all over. Set aside to cool and peel once they are cool enough to handle. Cut off the stem and finely chop the chillies. Mix the chillies in a bowl with the chopped garlic, oil and salt. The harissa will keep in a sealed container in the refrigerator for up to 1 week.

CHAPTER 2

PITAS

Filled pitas are, of course, a classic food in Israel. A few of the recipes in this chapter are traditionally associated with street food, such as falafel and sabich, but others are my own interpretation of dishes that just lend themselves perfectly to being stuffed into bread; the pita absorbs the juices from the food and becomes saturated with flavour.

As a kid, I used to love eating chargrilled pork neck in pita with hummus – the restaurant would cut the outer meat and continue to grill the remaining meat on the bone once they'd served the pita, then they would bring it out to you halfway through to eat the remaining meat from it.

Source the freshest, fluffiest pita you can, as it will make all the difference.

FALAFEL, TAHINI AND SALAD

Makes 2

2 pitas
300 g (10½ oz) Green Falafel
 (page 142)
6 tablespoons Chopped
 Salad (page 170)
6 tablespoons Classic Tahini
 (page 60) or shop-bought

A classic street food and perhaps the most ubiquitous of filled pitas. I developed this recipe when I was consulting on the deli offering of a popular food store in London; a good falafel is crunchy on the outside and very soft on the inside. It has a certain density but should still have a lightness to it – it just has so much texture in one bite. Falafel is one of the first things I eat when I go home.

Make the falafel according to the recipe on page 142. Make a slit in the top of the pitas of about 5 cm (2 in) so you can open it and fill them. Layer the pitas with some falafel balls, chopped salad and tahini and repeat until the pitas are full. Enjoy.

SABICH

Serves 2

2 eggs
1 large aubergine (eggplant),
    skin removed and cut in
    half widthwise, then cut
    into 1 cm (½ in)-thick slices
sea salt
about 500 ml (17 fl oz)
    vegetable oil
2 pitas
6 tablespoons Classic Tahini
    (page 60) or shop-bought
6 tablespoons Chopped
    Salad (page 170)
2 tablespoons amba (see
    introduction on page 54)
2 tablespoons finely
    chopped flat-leaf
    parsley leaves

This has been a staple street food in Israel since the 1960s, when it was made popular by Iraqi Jewish immigrants. There are big debates on the origin of this dish, and many iterations and interpretations. One such thought is that sabich originates from the word 'subeh', which means 'morning' in Arabic – it was something that you'd usually eat at the beginning of the day, often serving it with eggs and other breakfast items, but someone had the idea of serving it in a pita – and the rest is history.

Place the eggs in a small saucepan, cover with cold water, then bring to the boil and simmer for 8–10 minutes. Remove the eggs from the heat and cool under cold running water. Make sure the eggs are cooled down thoroughly otherwise you won't be able to peel them easily.

Lay the slices of aubergine on a tray in a single layer, then sprinkle with fine sea salt. Let sit for 30 minutes until the slices have released some of their liquid. Pat the aubergine dry with paper towel.

Heat the oil in a frying pan (skillet) over a medium heat to 180°C (360°F), then fry the aubergine slices for 3–4 minutes on each side until golden brown. (The aubergine slices should fry in one layer, so you might need to fry them in batches.) Remove from the heat.

Now you can assemble the pita. Make a slit in the top of the pitas of about 5 cm (2 in) so you can open it and fill them. Start with 2 tablespoons of tahini spread evenly inside. Slice the hard-boiled eggs and spread the slices out inside the pita. Follow with a couple of slices of aubergine and some salad and continue until the pita is full. Top with the remaining tahini and drizzle with amba. Finish with the chopped parsley.

OREN

GRILLED MACKEREL WITH TZATZIKI AND SPICY TOMATO SALAD

Serves 2

olive oil, for frying
2 mackerel fillets, about
    160 g (5½ oz) each (skin on)
4 tablespoons Tzatziki
    (page 20)
2 pitas

For the spicy tomato salad
2 large tomatoes, diced
    and strained of excess
    water
¼ small red onion,
    finely chopped
1 small, mild red chilli,
    finely chopped
2 tablespoons finely
    chopped coriander
    (cilantro) leaves
    and some stalks
1 tablespoon extra-virgin
    olive oil
1 teaspoon lemon juice
sea salt and freshly ground
    black pepper

Mackerel works so well in a pita because it's quite a fatty fish – you need to cook it skin-side down to get that lovely crispy skin, which creates a great textural contrast with the softness of the pita. Be sure to strain the tomatoes so your pita doesn't go soggy.

To make the spicy tomato salad, combine all the ingredients in a mixing bowl.

Heat a little olive oil a heavy frying pan (skillet) over a high heat, add the mackerel skin side down and fry for 3–4 minutes until the skin is crisp. Flip the fillets over and cook for another minute. Remove from the heat.

Make a slit in the top of the pitas of about 5 cm (2 in) so you can open it and fill them. Spread 2 tablespoons of tzatziki evenly inside each pita. Cut each fillet in half and place in the pita and add the spicy tomato salad.

GRILLED CHICKEN THIGHS WITH PILPELCHUMA, TAHINI AND WATERCRESS

Serves 2

1 tablespoon olive oil, plus
  extra for drizzling
sea salt and freshly ground
  black pepper
2 chicken thigh, deboned
  with skin on
2 tablespoons Pilpelchuma
  (page 28)
2 pitas
2 handfuls of watercress
a squeeze of lemon juice
6 tablespoons Classic Tahini
  (page 60) or shop-bought

This is truly delicious, offering such a great combination of flavours. In this recipe I use chicken thighs rather than breast, as they're much juicier and have more flavour. Try to get that skin good and crispy: cook them skin-side down to begin with, then flip over just to finish. The spicy pilpelchuma works perfectly with the chicken, and is nicely finished with the peppery watercress and rich tahini.

Season the chicken thighs all over with salt and pepper. Heat the oil in a heavy frying pan (skillet) and cook the chicken thighs skin-side down for 3–5 minutes, until golden brown and the skin is crisp. Turn and cook for a further 3–5 minutes, or until the chicken is fully cooked through.

Make a slit in the top of the pitas of about 5 cm (2 in) so you can open it and fill them. Spread the pipelchuma evenly inside the pita pockets. Insert the chicken thighs. Season the watercress with lemon juice, olive oil and salt and pepper, and stuff it inside the pita. Pour 3 tablespoons of tahini into each pita and serve.

LAMB AND BEEF ARAYES

Serves 2–4 as a starter

2 pitas
150 g (5½ oz) minced
   (ground) beef
100 g (3½ oz) minced
   (ground) lamb
½ white onion, diced
25 g (1 oz) parsley, leaves,
   finely chopped
25 g (1 oz) coriander
   (cilantro), finely chopped
¼ teaspoon ground cumin
¼ teaspoon sea salt
50 g (1¾ oz) lamb fat, melted
Classic Tahini (page 60)
   or shop-bought, to serve

This is a real eat-with-your-hands dish. The stuffed pita is usually cooked over charcoal, and you still get the absorbent effect of the pita – the bread inside soaks up all the meaty flavour and the outside is charred, smoky and crisp.

Preheat the oven to 180°C (350°F/gas 4).

Prepare a charcoal grill or preheat a griddle pan over a medium heat.

Make a slit in the top of the pitas of about 5 cm (2 in) so you can open it and fill them. Don't make the hole bigger as the recipe won't work. Mix all the ingredients (except the lamb fat and tahini) together in a bowl with your hands until well incorporated. Fill up the pitas with the mixture and, when full, press on the pitas to flatten them. Brush with lamb fat on both sides and grill over charcoal or fry on the hot griddle pan for about 5 minutes on each side, then place in the oven for 6–8 minutes. Remove the pita from the oven and cut into quarters. Serve with tahini on the side.

PULLED LAMB SHAWARMA WITH TAHINI AND YOGHURT DRESSING AND HERB SALAD

Serves 2

100 g (3½ oz) Classic Tahini (page 60 or shop-bought
100 g (3½ oz) Greek yoghurt
2 pitas
300 g (10½ oz) Slow-roast Leg of Lamb, Shawarma Style (page 220)
sea salt and freshly ground black pepper

For the herb salad
5 g (¼ oz) picked coriander (cilantro) leaves
5 g (¼ oz) flat-leaf parsley leaves
2 g mint
½ small red onion, sliced
2 tablespoons extra-virgin olive oil

This is such a great way to use the soft and juicy Slow-roast Leg of Lamb, Shawarma Style on page 220: you can just tuck it into a pita with a fragrant salad and dressing and enjoy. Here, the tahini and Greek yoghurt works really well together and add to the already robust flavour of the lamb, while the herb salad brings a hit of freshness.

To make the herb salad, combine all the ingredients in a mixing bowl and season with salt and pepper.

Reheat the pulled lamb shawarma in a saucepan over a medium heat until heated through.

Mix the tahini and yoghurt together in a bowl to make the dressing.

Make a slit in the top of the pitas of about 5 cm (2 in) so you can open it and fill them. Fill the pitas with the warmed lamb shawarma, tahini yoghurt dressing and the herb salad.

JERUSALEM MIX GRILL
WITH TAHINI AND AMBA

Serves 4

200 g (7 oz) boneless and
　skinless chicken thighs,
　cut into 1 cm (½ in) cubes
200 g (7 oz) duck (or chicken)
　hearts, halved and excess
　fat and blood removed
100 g (3½ oz) chicken liver,
　cleaned, trimmed to
　remove connective tissues
　and cut into 1 cm (½ in)
　cubes
1 teaspoon ground turmeric
1 tablespoon sweet paprika
2½ teaspoons ground cumin
vegetable oil, for frying
2 medium onions, cut into
　2 mm (¹⁄₁₆ in)-thick slices
sea salt

To serve
4 pita breads
12 tablespoons Classic Tahini
　(page 60) or shop-bought
4 tablespoons amba

Although it's not as common as something like falafel, this kind of mixed grill is a street-food staple in the Machne Yehuda market in Jerusalem. The traditional dish would usually be made with chicken hearts, liver and spleen; spleen isn't really available in the UK, so I've left it out and opted for duck hearts, which are plumper and have a gamier flavour that adds depth to the dish. Before opening Oren, I made this for a while at pop-ups and residencies, and it's now become a permanent fixture on the restaurant menu as it's so popular. Amba is a fermented mango condiment spiced with fenugreek, turmeric and chilli. It originated in Iraq and was brought to Israel by Jewish Iraqis. You can find it online or in specialist stores. You only need a little, as it can be overpowering.

Combine all the meat and offal in a mixing bowl, add the ground spices and mix well. Store in the refrigerator for a few hours or overnight.

Take the meat out of the refrigerator a couple of hours before cooking. Heat a cast-iron flat griddle pan (skillet) over a high heat until it smokes, then add a drizzle of vegetable oil followed by the sliced onions. Cook the onions for 3–5 minutes until golden brown, transfer to a plate and heat the pan again until smoking. Add some oil, followed by some of the meat and offal, and spread it out evenly (do not try to cook all the meat at once – it is essential that meat is cooked evenly in a single layer). Cook the meat for 6–7 minutes until the chicken thigh is no longer pink and all the meat is cooked through. Season with salt and then add the onions.

Cut open the edge of a pita to create a pocket, fill with 2 tablespoons of tahini and fill with some of the meats. Add another tablespoon of the tahini on top and a tablespoon of the amba. Eat immediately, preferably standing.

CHAPTER 3

TAHINI

Tahini is so much a part of the way I cook and eat. Whether it's drizzled on salads, meats or vegetable dishes, or generously scooped into pieces of warm pita, to me there aren't many things that aren't improved by it. I can eat it by the spoonful, and everyone in the kitchen at Oren from the head chef to the kitchen porter is addicted too.

Good tahini is sweet, with a mellow roast on the sesame seeds; we use Har Bracha tahini, which comes from a village called Nablus that is known for making one of the best tahinis. It's stoneground in small batches by a local Samaritan family who have dedicated themselves to making the best tahini possible. If you can source tahini from the town of Nablus, then you know you're getting great stuff.

CLASSIC TAHINI

Makes about 450 g (1 lb)

240 g (8½ oz) Classic Tahini
(page 60) or shop-bought
about 200 ml
(7 fl oz/⅔ cups)
cold water
2 teaspoons lemon juice
½ garlic clove, crushed
¼ teaspoon fine sea salt

You don't want to hide the tahini under too much garlic, lemon or salt. Sometimes I don't even add salt because it isn't needed. Taste as you go and adjust the seasoning accordingly. Some people add much more lemon and garlic to their tahini than I do, but I think that's because they're using an inferior brand. If you have a good-quality tahini, you barely need to add anything. It should be delicious as it is.

Put the tahini into a mixing bowl and start adding the cold water, a third at a time, while mixing with a whisk or spoon. When it has a smooth creamy consistency, add the lemon juice, garlic and salt. The tahini sauce can be stored in the refrigerator, but starts to lose depth of flavour after a day, so always make it fresh.

HUMMUS

Makes about 1 kg (2 lb 4 oz)

600 g (1 lb 5 oz) dried
  chickpeas (garbanzos),
  soaked in plenty of water
  for 24 hours
1 teaspoon bicarbonate
  of soda
1 teaspoon sea salt
75 ml (2½ fl oz/⅓ cup)
  lemon juice
200 g (7 oz) Classic Tahini
  (page 60) or shop-bought

Don't be tempted to cut corners here – it's worth it to follow every step, just as I've laid out. You might think using tinned chickpeas (garbanzos) is quicker, but you won't get the same result. Try to choose smaller chickpeas if you can; they are more suitable for hummus and give a creamier finish. You really do need a food processor for this one, and it will be working hard.

Rinse the chickpeas for a few minutes, then drain and place in a stockpot with enough water to cover. Add the bicarbonate of soda, bring to the boil and simmer for about 2 hours, or until the chickpeas are soft enough to yield easily when pinched. Drain, saving 125 ml (4¼ fl oz/generous ½ cup) of the cooking liquid. Leave the chickpeas to cool slightly, then transfer to a food processor and blitz for 3–4 minutes. Add the cooking liquid and blitz for a further 2 minutes. Add the salt, lemon juice and tahini and blitz for another 2 minutes. Store in the refrigerator. It will keep for up to 3 days.

FRIED CAULIFLOWER FLORETS
WITH TAHINI AND GRATED TOMATOES

Serves 4

3 large tomatoes
sea salt
1 large cauliflower,
    separated into small
    (2–3 cm/¾–1¼ in) florets
500 ml (17 fl oz/generous
    2 cups) vegetable oil,
    for frying
150 g (5½ oz) Classic Tahini
    (page 60) or shop-bought
25 g (1 oz) flat-leaf parsley,
    coarsely chopped

You'll find this served in a lot of seafood restaurants in Tel Aviv, as it makes a great side dish for fish. I like to serve this straight away, when it's hot and freshly cooked. It's great as part of a mezze spread, as it's perfect for sharing. Grating the tomatoes maximises their flavour while minimising excess liquid giving a concentrated taste that sits perfectly with the tahini here.

Grate the tomatoes on the coarse side of a cheese grater and transfer to a fine sieve. Strain until there is no liquid in the tomatoes and season to taste with salt.

Bring a large pan of water to the boil and add a tablespoon of salt. Add the florets and cook for 3–4 minutes, then drain and leave in the colander with the stems facing up until completely dry.

Heat the oil in a deep-frying pan (skillet) to 180°C (360°F). Gently transfer a small batch of the florets into the hot oil and fry for 5–6 minutes until golden brown. Transfer to a plate lined with paper and continue with the rest and sprinkle with salt while hot.

Arrange the fried cauliflower florets on a plate, drizzle with the tahini and scatter with grated tomatoes and the chopped parsley.

CHOPPED ROMAINE LETTUCE WITH RADISHES, SPRING ONION, DILL AND TAHINI

Serves 4

2 large romaine lettuce
   hearts (only the white part)
4 spring onions (scallions),
   thinly sliced (using the
   whole length of the onions)
25 g (1 oz) dill, finely chopped
1 large red radish (or any
   other spicy/sharp radish),
   cut into thin strips
25 ml (¾ fl oz) extra-virgin
   olive oil
juice of 1 lemon
sea salt
100 g (3½ oz) Classic Tahini
   (page 60) or shop-bought

This is a very refreshing salad, with such a great combination of flavours. It can be enjoyed as a starter or a side served with meat or fish, but I'll gladly eat a bowlful on its own. You only want to use the white crunchy part of the Romaine lettuce here – you don't need the green outer leaves. Submerging the lettuce in ice-cold water really brings out the crispiness, but do make sure you drain it well in the salad spinner, as nobody wants a soggy salad. Follow every stage of this recipe closely to make this dish sing.

Separate the romaine lettuce leaves from the stem and place in a bowl with ice-cold water for 15 minutes.

Using a salad spinner, dry out the lettuce, then cut it into thin strips with a sharp knife and place in a mixing bowl. Add the spring onions, dill and radish. Drizzle with the olive oil and lemon juice, season with salt and toss gently.

Spread the tahini on a plate then arrange the salad on top.

CRISPY SARDINES WITH GREEN TAHINI

Serves 4

500 ml (17 fl oz/generous
    2 cups) vegetable oil,
    for frying
6 sardines, gutted and
    scaled (80 g/2¾ oz each)
lemon wedges, to serve

For the green tahini
50 g (1¾ oz) Classic Tahini
    (page 60) or shop-bought
35 ml (1¼ fl oz) cold water
1 garlic clove, finely grated
juice of ½ lemon
2 tablespoons chopped
    coriander (cilantro)
2 tablespoons chopped
    flat-leaf parsley

For the seasoned flour
250 g (9 oz/2 cups) plain
    (all-purpose) flour
6 g (¼ oz) cornflour
    (cornstarch)
5 g (¼ oz) sea salt
¼ teaspoon crushed black
    pepper
½ teaspoon sweet paprika
¼ teaspoon ground cumin

Note
The seasoned flour makes
too much for the recipe,
but it makes it easier
to coat the sardines.

This green tahini is simple to make, but it's definitely not subtle. With lots of fresh green herbs, garlic and lemon, it's pungent and has a real kick. It pairs really well with crunchy fried food, and can stand up to the bold flavours of these crispy sardines. It would also work well with squid.

Tip: make sure your frying oil is up to temperature before adding the fish to get that nice crispy finish.

To make the green tahini, combine the tahini and herbs in a bowl. Add the lemon juice and season with salt to taste.

For the seasoned flour, combine all the ingredients in a bowl.

Heat the oil in a saucepan to 180°C (360°F). Dip the sardines in water then transfer to the seasoned flour and coat the fish with flour, pressing the flour on the fish with your hands. The sardines should be completely coated with flour. Gently drop the fish into the hot oil and fry for about 2 minutes until crispy and golden. (Do not overcrowd the pan – fry in batches if necessary.) Fry the sardines for 2 minutes, until golden. Transfer the fried fish to a tray lined with paper towel and sprinkle with sea salt flakes. Serve with the green tahini and lemon wedges.

AGED BEEF ONGLET WITH TAHINI AND ROAST CHILLI HARISSA

**Serves 2 as a main;
4 as a starter**

350 g (12 oz) aged onglet,
    cut into 2 cm (¾ in) pieces
sea salt
50 g (1¾ oz) Classic Tahini
    (page 60) or shop-bought

For the roast chilli harissa
4 mild red chillies
    (50 g/1¾ oz)
1 garlic clove, finely chopped
2 tablespoons olive oil
¼ teaspoon sea salt

This is a great example of letting good ingredients speak for themselves, and the combination of flavours here is delicious. Onglet is quite a rich cut, almost offally in flavour due to its iron content, so it really is best cooked over charcoal, where the smoky coals can enhance its natural flavour. I used to serve it in the restaurant on a big skewer, with lots of tahini and chilli harissa on the side.

Preheat a charcoal grill.

Either wooden or metal skewers can be used. If using wooden skewers, start by soaking the wooden skewers overnight in water, to prevent them from burning. Alternatively, use metal skewers, which don't need to be soaked.

To make the harissa, roast the chillies over an open flame (either gas or barbecue), until blackened all over, then set aside to cool. Peel and discard the skin and finely chop the flesh of the chillies, keeping the seeds. Combine the chillies with the garlic, oil and salt.

Thread the meat onto skewers and season generously with salt. Grill the onglet skewers for about 3 minutes on each side – the onglet is best eaten medium rare.

Serve with tahini and roast chilli harissa.

CHAPTER 4

PRESERVED LEMONS

If you go to a market in Israel, among the jars of different kinds of pickles, you'll find huge jars of preserved lemons. They're a key ingredient and are used in everything from sandwiches and salads to marinades. Home cooks use them to bring out the flavours in stuffed vegetables and koftas, or add them to stocks to impart their unique taste. You only need a small amount – if you use too much, the flavour can be overpowering, changing the balance of the whole recipe. Used sparingly, they bring complex structure to a dish, adding an extraordinary depth of flavour.

Note: The longer they sit in the preserving jar, the sweeter they become – a one-month preserved lemon will have a different flavour to one that has been preserved for four or five months. The older ones will be almost like a jam, and you can use the whole thing, but if you're using a younger preserved lemon, be sure to discard the pulp, as it will be bitter.

PRESERVED LEMONS

Makes 3 litre (34 fl oz/4 cups) jar

200 g (7 oz) rock salt
10 unwaxed lemons, washed
    and cut into 2 cm (¾ in)-thick
    slices
10 garlic cloves, bashed
10 bay leaves
250 ml (8½ fl oz/1 cup) lemon
    juice

You can, of course, buy preserved lemons, but I think they taste much better if you make them yourself. It's a very simple process – you simply salt the lemons, then layer them in jars with garlic, bay leaves and lemon juice. After that, you need only time and patience – they should be left to ferment for at least two months. I've given instructions for sliced preserved lemons, which is quicker than leaving them whole.

Tip the salt onto a flat tray then tap the lemon slices in the salt on each side. Arrange the salted lemon slices in sterilised jars, layering the garlic and bay leaves between the lemon slices. Cover the lemons with the lemon juice and seal the jar, making sure that the lemon slices are covered with juice. Set on a shelf away from direct sunlight and leave to ferment for at least 2 months. Once open, the preserved lemons keep well in the refrigerator for 6 months or more.

FRESH BROAD BEANS WITH SLOW-ROAST TOMATOES AND PRESERVED LEMON

Serves 4

1 kg (2 lb 4 oz) fresh broad (fava) beans, podded
50 g (1¾ oz) Preserved Lemon (page 78), roughly chopped
extra-virgin olive oil, for drizzling
sea salt and freshly ground black pepper
oregano, leaves only, chopped, to garnish

For the vegetable stock
1 white onion, peeled and cut into 2 cm (¾ in) chunks
2 celery stalks, washed and cut into 2 cm (¾ in) chunks
1 large leek, washed and cut into 2 cm (¾ in) chunks
1 medium fennel bulb, washed and cut into 2 cm (¾ in) chunks
2 garlic cloves
2 bay leaves
½ teaspoon allspice berries
4 litres (135 fl oz/17 cups) water
¼ teaspoon sea salt
1 tablespoon olive oil

For the slow-roast tomatoes
2 large, ripe tomatoes
4 sprigs of thyme
2 tablespoons olive oil

Pure, green, refreshing – delicious. This takes a bit of effort, but the end result is so worth it: the perfect spring dish, celebrating fresh ingredients. The freshness is really key here, so I wouldn't attempt to make it with frozen broad (fava) beans. And take care not to overcook them: you really want to keep that crunch and freshness. The preserved lemons add an umami and depth to the clean flavours, giving the dish a kick and providing complexity. I like this served warm or at room temperature, not necessarily piping hot.

The quantities here will make more broth than you need for this recipe, but the leftovers make a great base for a soup or any stock-based dish. The broth can be frozen for up to three months.

To make the vegetable broth, put the vegetables in a stockpot with the rest of the ingredients. Bring to the boil, then reduce the heat so the broth is simmering. Simmer for 1½–2 hours, until you get 250 ml (8½ fl oz) of liquid, then strain.

To make the slow-roast tomatoes, preheat the oven to 160°C (315°F/gas 2). Cut each tomato into six pieces and place in a mixing bowl with the thyme sprigs, a pinch of salt and pepper, and olive oil. Toss gently and place on an oven tray lined with baking parchment. Roast in the oven for about 1½ hours, or until the tomatoes have shrunken by a third, have a deep red colour and are slightly charred.

Prepare a bowl of iced water. Bring a small saucepan of salted water to the boil, add the podded beans and cook for 45 seconds, then transfer to the bowl of iced water. Remove the thick grey skin around the beans by squeezing them with your fingers.

Reheat the vegetable stock, then add the beans, preserved lemon, a couple of tablespoons of oil and warm for 1–2 minutes.

Place in serving bowls, top with the slow-roast tomatoes, oregano leaves and drizzle with some more olive oil.

HOMEMADE GRAVLAX WITH LABNEH AND PRESERVED LEMON

Serves 8–10

1.8 kg (4 lb) side of salmon
100 g (3½ oz) dill, finely
    chopped, to garnish
200 g (7 oz) Labneh
    (page 16)
50 g (1¾ oz) Preserved
    Lemon (page 78),
    roughly chopped
extra-virgin olive oil,
    for drizzling

For the cure
250 g (9 oz/1¼ cups) caster
    (superfine) sugar
250 g (9 oz) coarse sea salt
10 g (¼ oz) green cardamom
    pods, crushed
15 g (½ oz) fennel seeds
20 g (¾ oz) sweet paprika

I've been making this recipe for 20 years, and it's a bit of a playful take on the classic flavour combination of smoked salmon, cream cheese and lemon. Here, we use labneh and preserved lemon for richer, rounder flavours, and the cure is floral and fragrant, giving a very different result to your average gravlax. It's rewarding to make and feels a bit special, so it's an ideal dish to serve when you have guests. You will need to allow 36–48 hours for curing.

Combine all the ingredients for the salmon cure in a mixing bowl until well incorporated. Lay the side of salmon, skin-side down, in a deep tray and cover it with the cure mixture. Cover with cling film (plastic wrap) and place in the refrigerator for 36–48 hours, depending on the thickness of the fish and how dry you want it to be.

Rinse the fish with cold water and pat dry with a clean cloth or kitchen towel. Cover with the chopped dill a couple of hours before serving and cut into 2 mm (¹⁄₁₆ in)-thick slices. Serve with a dollop of labneh, preserved lemon and drizzle with extra-virgin olive oil. Once cured, the gravlax will keep for 2 days in the refrigerator in an airtight container.

 OREN

FISH KEBABS WITH PRESERVED LEMON AND TZATZIKI

Serves 3

For the fish kebabs
350 g (12 oz) filleted hake,
    cut into 5 mm (¼ in) dice
130 g (4½ oz) white onion,
    finely chopped
30 g (1 oz) flat-leaf parsley
    leaves, finely chopped
30 g (1 oz) coriander
    (cilantro), finely chopped
¼ teaspoon ground cumin
¼ teaspoon ground
    coriander
30 g (1 oz) Preserved Lemon
    (page 78), finely chopped
¼ teaspoon sea salt
10 g (¼ oz) olive oil, plus
    extra for grilling and
    drizzling

For the tzatziki
200 g (7 oz) cucumber
2 garlic cloves
250 g (9 oz) Labneh
    (page 16)
sea salt
juice of ½ lemon

I've been making this recipe for fifteen years, maybe more, and it remains a firm favourite. Whenever we put it on the menu at the restaurant, it sells really fast. Unlike fish cakes, these kebabs contain no egg, flour or breadcrumbs as a binding agent, and people often ask how the mixture holds together. The secret is in the 'slapping' process used when mixing, so don't be tempted to skip this step. We grill the kebabs over charcoal for a lovely smokiness, but they can be made in a frying pan (skillet) or griddle pan. The tzatziki adds a clean element that sits perfectly with the robust flavours of the fish kebabs.

Hake works really well for this dish, but most firm white fish would do. The most important thing is that the fish must be super fresh.

Combine the diced fish, onion, chopped herbs and preserved lemon in a mixing bowl. Add the spices, preserved lemons, salt and the olive oil. Mix with your hands in a 'slapping' movement by grabbing the mixture and slapping it against the inside of the bowl repeatedly until it starts to come together (this will add elasticity to the mixture and give the fish a better texture once cooked). Form into 50 g (1¾ oz) kebabs/cylinders and transfer to the refrigerator to cool for a couple of hours.

Preheat a charcoal grill (or you can use a griddle pan). Rub the kebabs with olive oil and grill for 2–3 minutes on each side or until the kebabs have firmed up and are cooked through.

For the tzatziki, finely chop the cucumbers and squeeze them to lose any excess liquids. Finely grate the garlic, add all the ingredients to the bowl and season with lemon juice and salt if needed.

Serve with a generous dollop of tzatziki and drizzle with olive oil.

GRILLED TAMWORTH PORK CHOP WITH CHARRED GARLIC AND PRESERVED LEMON

Serves 2

450 g (1 lb) Tamworth pork
　chop (or other free-range
　pork chop)
10 g (¼ oz) Preserved
　Lemon (page 75),
　roughly chopped
sea salt

For the confit garlic
4 whole garlic bulbs
200 ml (7 fl oz/scant 1 cup)
　olive oil
2 bay leaves
10 g (½ oz) thyme sprigs

This recipe means a lot to me. When I was a child, my dad took me to a fifty-year-old steakhouse in Tel Aviv, where they served their grilled pork chops smothered in crushed raw garlic. The menus at these types of steakhouses have such broad influences; an aubergine (eggplant) salad with Romanian heritage sits alongside hummus that has been made in the same small village just outside of the city for fifty years, and for dessert, you'll find German Bavarian cream – for me, this is exactly what the food of Tel Aviv is all about.

You need to choose a good-quality, free-range, rare-breed pork for this dish. If you can't get Tamworth chops, ask your butcher for advice on what to use.

Preheat the oven to 180°C (350°F/gas 3). To make the confit garlic, cut 5 mm (¼ in) from the bottom of the garlic bulbs and lay them on a roasting tray (pan) cut-side down. Pour the olive oil over the garlic, add the bay leaves and thyme, covered the tray with foil, and roast in the oven for 20–25 minutes until the garlic is slightly browned. Remove from the oven, let the garlic cool down, then squeeze the cloves out of their skins and cover with the olive oil and herbs. The garlic will keep for 2 weeks in the refrigerator in a sealed jar, covered with oil.

If using a charcoal grill to cook the pork, then first preheat until the coals are white; alternatively, heat a griddle plan over a high heat. Season the pork chop generously with sea salt on both sides and grill the chop for 5–7 minutes on one side, then turn and grill on the other side for 4–6 minutes. The pork is done when it has a light pink colour in the middle before resting. Remove from the grill and set aside on a tray or a plate to rest for 7–8 minutes.

In a small saucepan, heat 6–8 garlic cloves, and the preserved lemon, with about ½ teaspoon of confit garlic oil.

Carve the rested pork off the bone into 1 cm (½ in)-thick slices.

Sprinkle with sea salt and drizzle the garlic and preserved lemon over the pork.

OREN

BARBECUED, MARINATED SPATCHCOCKED QUAIL WITH PRESERVED LEMON SALSA VERDE

Serves 2

2 spatchcocked quails
sea salt

For the marinade

3½ tablespoons Pernod
25 ml (2 tablespoons) olive oil
20 g (¾ oz) oregano leaves,
    picked
50 g (¾ oz) honey
4 garlic cloves, crushed

For the salsa verde

3 garlic cloves
5 tinned anchovy fillets, in oil
2 teaspoons capers
20 g (¾ oz) Preserved
    Lemon (page 78)
50 g (1¾ oz) flat-leaf parsley,
    finely chopped with stalks
    discarded
30 g (1 oz) basil, finely
    chopped with stalks
    discarded
15 g (½ oz) oregano, finely
    chopped with stalks
    discarded
15 g (½ oz) mint, finely
    chopped with stalks
    removed
1 teaspoon Dijon mustard
1½ tablespoons white
    wine vinegar
150 ml (5 fl oz/⅔ cup)
    olive oil
sea salt and freshly ground
    black pepper

A Pernod-based marinade, charcoal-charred skin and a punch of preserved lemon means this dish is a real festival of flavour. Spatchcocking the quail is a vital step here: it gives the meat a greater surface area, meaning you can quickly cook the bird without any parts of it drying out, resulting in delicious, succulent meat. The marinade helps with this, too, as the alcohol cures the meat slightly, helping it cook more quickly and evenly, as well as lending it a slight aniseed flavour. I really recommend you cook this over the barbecue to get that lovely, charred finish. The accompanying salsa verde is quite a classic recipe, but the addition of preserved lemon, which pairs so well with poultry, adds depth and a kick.

Tip. This could also be made with poussin.

Combine all the marinade ingredients, put the quails in a container and pour the marinade over the quails. Rub the marinade into the quails, then cover and allow to marinate in the refrigerator for 24 hours.

To make the salsa verde, first finely chop the garlic with the anchovies, capers and preserved lemon, then put in a bowl with all the remaining ingredients and mix to combine. Season to taste with salt and pepper.

Take the quails out of the refrigerator 2 hours before cooking and remove the excess marinade with paper towel (keeping the marinade aside for brushing when grilling).

Preheat a charcoal grill. Grill the quails for 4–5 minutes on each side, brushing them occasionally with the marinade. The quails should be cooked until pink close to the leg bone – do not overcook them as this will make them tough and dry to eat. Sprinkle with sea salt and a generous amount of the salsa verde. Eat with your fingers.

STONE-BAKED FLATBREADS WITH CURED SARDINES AND PRESERVED LEMON

Serves 4

1 small red onion, thinly sliced
sea salt
extra-virgin olive oil,
   for drizzling

For the flatbreads
250 ml (8½ fl oz/1 cup)
   lukewarm water
315 g (11 oz/2½ cups) '00' flour
35 g (1¼ oz) semolina flour
pinch of sugar
⅛ teaspoon active dried
   yeast
1 teaspoon olive oil
¼ teaspoon sea salt

To garnish
12 Cured Sardines (page 192)
1 teaspoons finely chopped
   Preserved Lemon
   (page 78)

This dish makes a nice starter when you have guests over: it feels quite simple, but has complex flavours. When we make flatbreads at the restaurant we use a pizza oven, but I've given instructions for using a pizza stone in a domestic oven – you won't get quite the same result, but it will still be delicious.

To make the flatbread dough, pour the water into the bowl of a stand mixer fitted with the dough hook, add the flours, sugar, yeast and olive oil, and mix on low speed for 2 minutes, then add the salt. (Alternatively, mix the ingredients in a bowl and then knead by hand for about 20 minutes.) Continue mixing on a slow speed for 15 minutes until the dough is elastic. It should be very soft and still a bit sticky. Transfer the dough to a large container with a lid and prove for 24–48 hours in the refrigerator. You can leave the dough in the refrigerator for up to 4 days to develop the flavour.

Take the dough out of the refrigerator 4–5 hours before baking. Cut the dough into four pieces. With floured hands, form the dough into balls. Place on a tray without any flour, leaving space between them, and cover with a dish towel to prove at room temperature for about 3 hours, or until the dough has doubled in size.

To bake the flatbreads, you can either use a stone pizza oven or a pizza stone in a domestic oven. If using a pizza oven, preheat it to 350°C (660°F). Using a dough scraper, place a ball of dough onto a '00'-floured surface. Press the dough with both hands from the centre to the edge to deflate the dough. Turn the piece of dough and repeat this process on the other side, then lift the dough and stretch it between your fingers until the dough is about 25 cm (10 in) long and 10 cm (4 in) wide. Scatter some onion slices and salt over the flatbread. Drizzle with a bit of olive oil. Using a pizza peel or a wooden board, slide the dough into the hot oven and bake for about 2 minutes, or until the bread has risen and developed a nice golden-brown colour.

If you are using a domestic oven with a stone, preheat your oven to its maximum temperature with the stone inside for 1 hour before baking. Repeat the process above and bake the flatbread for 4–5 minutes or until risen and golden-brown. Repeat to bake the remaining bread.

While the flatbreads are still warm, lay each flatbread with three sardine fillets and some chopped preserved lemon, sprinkle with sea salt and drizzle with olive oil.

CHALLAH WITH PRESERVED LEMON AND ZA'ATAR

Makes 3 loaves

320 ml (11 fl oz/1 ⅓ cups)
   lukewarm water
30 g (1 oz) fresh yeast
   (or 15 g/½ oz active
   dried yeast)
800 g (1 lb 12 oz) plain
   (all-purpose) flour
2 large eggs, plus an extra
   egg (beaten) for egg wash
80 g (2¾ oz/generous ⅓ cup)
   caster (superfine) sugar
2 ⅛ teaspoon fine sea salt
60 g (2¼ oz/4 tablespoons)
   unsalted butter, melted
90 g (3¼ oz) Preserved
   Lemon (page 78),
   roughly chopped
3 tablespoons za'atar,
   to sprinkle

This recipe is inspired by the challah made by my extremely talented friend Uri Scheft, who runs Lehamim Bakery in Tel Aviv and founded Breads Bakery in New York. I've known him for fifteen years – I used to buy bread from him when I was head chef at a restaurant in Israel, and we've been friends ever since.

This recipe can be adapted to suit the foods you're serving it with, but the combination of preserved lemon and za'atar here is truly special, and the smell when it comes out of the oven is irresistible.

Pour the water into the bowl of a stand mixer fitted with the dough hook and crumble in the fresh yeast. (If using dried yeast, then it needs to be activated in water before being added.) To activate the yeast, place in a bowl with 50 ml (1¾ fl oz) of the total amount of water until bubbles start to appear.

Add the flour, eggs, sugar, salt and melted butter, and mix on a slow speed for 4 minutes, until incorporated. Add the chopped preserved lemons, increase the speed and mix for another 5 minutes until the dough is elastic. Remove the dough from the bowl and roll it into a ball.

Place the dough in a bowl, cover with a dish towel and let the dough rise at room temperature for 40 minutes, or until doubled in size.

Cut the dough into thirds and divide each third into three pieces. Roll each piece until it is 25 cm (10 in) long, then braid. To do this, on a clean surface, position three lengths of dough side by side and press the lengths together at the end furthest away from you so they hold in one piece. Braid the lengths into a plait, then press the bottom ends together to seal. Repeat with the remaining six lengths of dough to make three loaves. Arrange the three challah on a three baking sheets, cover with a dish towel and leave to prove in a warm place for 35 minutes or until doubled in size.

Preheat the oven to 170°C (325°F/gas 3). Brush the risen loaves with the beaten egg and sprinkle with 1 tablespoon of za'atar on each loaf. Bake in the for about 22 minutes, or until they are golden brown.

Remove from the oven and let the loaves cool for at least 1 hour before eating.

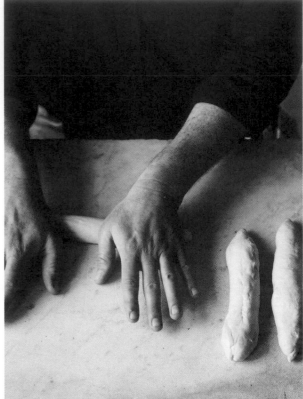

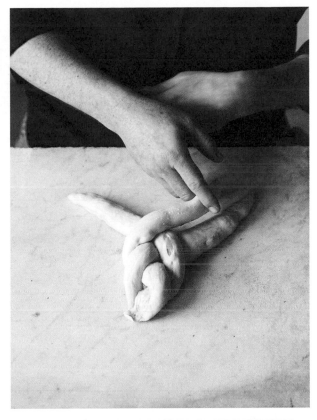

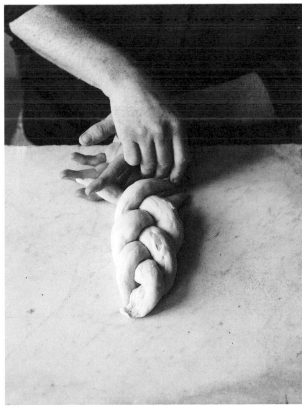

CHAPTER 5

TOMATOES

I really love tomatoes – this ingredient is home to me. They were a dominant part of the food I grew up with in Israel, and remain a key feature in the dishes that I prepare at the restaurant now. They are so versatile – they can be grilled, slow-roasted, sliced raw into salads – and every preparation reveals a different flavour, from sweet to acid to bold.

I feel lucky to have grown up in a sunny country where good-quality tomatoes are abundant, and every time I go back to visit, I'm amazed by the rich variety of fresh tomatoes available, many of which are grown in Arava in the south, close to the border with Jordan.

This is one of those ingredients where it really is worth spending more money and getting the best quality you can – they make all the difference to a dish. I find you can really taste the sun in them.

LIBYAN CHRAIME SAUCE

Makes about 500 ml
(17 fl oz/generous 2 cups)

3½ tablespoons vegetable oil
20 g (¾ oz) garlic cloves,
   grated
1½ tablespoons sweet
   paprika
1 tablespoon ground cumin
1½ tablespoons ground
   caraway seeds
1 teaspoon hot chilli powder
1 teaspoon fine sea salt
125 g (4½ oz/1 cup) tomato
   purée (paste)
400 ml (13 fl oz/generous
   1½ cups) water
25 ml (¾ fl oz) lemon juice

Chraime is a traditional Libyan fish dish. 'Chraime' means 'hot' in Arabic. I pair it with monkfish on page 208, but really it would suit all manner of grilled meat, fish or vegetables that have a bit of structure and bite.

Heat the oil in a saucepan over medium heat for 2–3 minutes. Add the garlic and cook for 3 minutes, then add all the spices and salt and reduce the heat to low. Stir for 3–4 minutes, still stirring occasionally. Add the tomato purée, keep stirring for a further 2 minutes, then start whisking in the water, a third at a time. Cook over a low heat for 35 minutes until the sauce has a sharp and distinct spice flavour and the spices don't taste raw anymore. Remove from the heat, stir in the lemon juice and leave to cool.

MATBUCHA

**Serves 4–6 as a starter
(appetiser)**

5 large, ripe tomatoes
70 ml (2⅓ fl oz/⅓ cup)
　vegetable oil
55 g (2 oz) green mild
　Turkish chilli (Sivri), cut
　into 5 mm (¼ in)-thick
　slices
20 g (¾ oz) (about 1–2 chillies)
mild Dutch red chillies, cut
　into 5 mm (¼ in)-thick
　slices
5 garlic cloves, roughly
　chopped
1 tablespoon sweet paprika
¾ teaspoon sea salt
½ teaspoon sugar

A classic Moroccan salad which featured almost on every meal
I had when I was kid. The name of this dish comes from the Arabic
for 'cooked'. The quality of the tomatoes is so important here, as
they are the real stars of the show. Cook matbutcha slowly – it
really needs plenty of time for the flavours to develop. Served
simply with bread, it's delicious as a mezze or starter, but you
could also use it in sandwiches, maybe paired with hummus or
some feta. It makes a great base for shakshuka as well. It's really
versatile.

Score the tomatoes with an 'X' using a sharp knife, and trim the
green parts from their tops. Prepare a bowl of iced water. Bring
a pan of water to the boil, then add the tomatoes and submerge
them for about 30 seconds until the skin starts to peel away.
Transfer the tomatoes to the iced water and remove their skin.

Heat the oil in a saucepan over a medium heat for 1 minute, then
add the chillies and garlic, reduce the heat to medium-low and fry
for 2–3 minutes, stirring frequently to avoid the garlic burning.

Coarsely chop the tomatoes and add them to the pan of chillies
and garlic, followed by the paprika, salt and sugar. Reduce the
heat to low and cook for 45 minutes, stirring occasionally. The
matbucha is ready when most (but not all) of the liquid has
evaporated. Remove from the heat and leave to cool.

Eat at room temperature with a slice of challah (page 100),
or anything you want really.

MARINDA TOMATOES, KALAMATA OLIVES AND PINE NUTS

Serves 4

6 Marinda tomatoes
12 Kalamata olives
   (not pitted)
½ red onion, thinly sliced
50 g (1¾ oz) coriander
   (cilantro), leaves picked
   and roughly chopped
4 tablespoons extra-virgin
   olive oil
25 g (1 oz) toasted pine nuts
sea salt and freshly ground
   black pepper

Marinda tomatoes are the best for this simple salad. A winter tomato with a firm skin, Marindas can feel quite tough to the touch and can look unripe, but when you slice them open, they are so sweet. I actually find winter tomatoes more delicious than summer tomatoes: for me, they pack in more flavour and sugar. If you can't get Marinda tomatoes, a Spanish Raf tomato would also be great. The important thing is that you want a good-quality tomato with texture and sweetness, nothing soggy or soft. Very few other ingredients are needed to make the salad sing.

Slice the tomatoes crossway into 1.5 cm (½ in) slices and place in a large mixing bowl. Remove the stones from the olives, leaving the olives in large pieces, and add to the bowl. Add the coriander to the bowl. Add the olive oil and pine nuts, season with salt and pepper, and toss gently. The salad should be eaten straight away.

GRILLED SQUID WITH CHOPPED TOMATOES, CHILLI AND CORIANDER

Serves 4

4 medium fresh squid,
   (about 100 g/3½ oz)

For the tomato salad
2 plum tomatoes, cut
   into 5 mm (¾ in) dice
2 mild red chillies, deseeded
   and finely diced
2 garlic cloves, finely
   chopped
½ bunch of coriander
   (cilantro) leaves and some
   of the stalks, chopped
olive oil, for drizzling
   and brushing
juice of ½ lemon
sea salt and freshly ground
   black pepper

Squid is one of my favourite kinds of seafood to eat and it needs very little intervention to be delicious. Here, the fresh chopped tomatoes complement the robust seafood flavours that are already present: two simple ingredients that combine to make something special with minimal effort.

Clean the squid, removing the intestines, cutting off the tentacles and removing the rest of the head.

Rinse the squid with cold water and pat dry with paper towels. Cut the tubes in half lengthwise on one side to open the squid up and remove any membrane by scraping with a spoon. Using a small, sharp knife, score in a crosshatch on the inside part of the tube, being careful to avoid cutting through to the other side.

Preheat a grill or griddle pan to high.

In the meantime, prepare the tomato salad. Combine the tomatoes, chillies, garlic and coriander in a bowl. Set aside and drizzle with olive oil and lemon juice, and season with salt and pepper, just before serving.

Lightly brush the squid and its tentacles with olive oil and grill for 1 minute on each side. Season with salt. Remove from the grill, transfer to plates and dress with the tomato salad.

WILD SEA BASS CRUDO WITH SHEEP'S YOGHURT AND TOMATOES

Serves 4

2 large ripe tomatoes,
    washed
200 g (7 oz) wild sea bass
    fillet (or any other firm
    white fish)
50 g (1¾ oz) sheep's yoghurt
    or Greek yoghurt
olive oil, for drizzling
juice of ½ lemon, plus extra
    to serve
sea salt flakes

This is a very simple recipe, but it's important to follow the method precisely for the best results. Grating tomatoes sounds simple enough, but it has a huge impact – you effectively extract the flavour of the tomato while straining off all the excess liquid. You are left with a flavour that's deeply concentrated but still very fresh. It's a great way to use tomatoes, and can be used in a variety of dishes (try serving grated tomatoes simply over pasta). As ever, the quality of the tomatoes is key. You could use another fish here, but go for a round fish rather than a flat one – something like sea bream or red snapper. You want your fish to be super fresh, and wild rather than farmed. Ask your fishmonger for the best fish that have been caught that day – this is always important when you're making a raw fish dish.

Grate the tomatoes into a bowl on the coarse side of a cheese grater, discarding the skin. Transfer to a fine sieve and let the water drain until completely dry. Season with salt.

Cut the fish into 2 mm (¹⁄₁₆ in)-thick slices and arrange on platter or individual plates. Generously add dollops of the grated tomatoes and yoghurt between the fish slices. Drizzle olive oil around and on the fish, followed by some lemon juice, and season the fish carefully with sea salt. Enjoy immediately with an extra wedge of lemon to serve.

BEEF AND LAMB KOFTAS
IN FRAGRANT TOMATO SAUCE

Serves about 6

For the tomato sauce
3½ tablespoons olive oil
12 large garlic cloves, peeled
75 g (2¾ oz) tomato purée
    (paste)
25 g (1 oz) ground cumin
25 g (1 oz) sweet paprika
1.5 kg (3 lb 5 oz) tinned whole
    tomatoes, chopped
20 g (¾ oz) sea salt
½ teaspoon cracked black
    pepper
25 g (1 oz) oregano sprigs
3 dried red chillies
    (optional)

For the koftas
500 g (1 lb 2 oz) minced
    (ground) beef
300 g (10½ oz) minced
    (ground) lamb
150 g (5½ oz) onions, diced
1 bunch of flat-leaf parsley
    (80 g/2¾ oz) leaves and
    some stalk, finely chopped
1 coriander (cilantro) bunch
    (80 g) leaves and some
    stalk, finely chopped
100 g (3½ oz) dried
    breadcrumbs
5 g (¼ oz) sea salt
6 g (¼ oz) ground cumin
2 tablespoons vegetable oil,
    for frying

To serve
steamed basmati rice
pitas
Classic Tahini (page 60)
    or shop-bought

Koftas with rice was something I and a lot of kids would eat after school; the original version I used to have as a child will always have a place in my heart, but the recipe here is much improved. The sauce is richer, and I use a combination of lamb and beef, which gives the koftas a more complex flavour.

First, make the tomato sauce. Heat the olive oil in a saucepan over a medium heat, add the whole garlic cloves and sauté, without letting them colour, for 4–5 minutes. Add the tomato purée and sauté for a further 2 minutes, then add the cumin and paprika, and stir over low heat. Add the chopped tomatoes, salt, pepper and the oregano (no need to pick the leaves). Bring the sauce to the boil, stirring occasionally, then reduce the heat to low and cook for 1 hour–1½ hours. The sauce is ready when most of the water has evaporated, but it should not be too thick. If using, add the dried chillies.

Make sure the meat is at room temperature before you make the koftas. Put the meat in large mixing bowl and add all the other ingredients, except the oil. Mix well with your hands until the mixture is evenly combined and there are no lumps of herbs in one area. Form into 20 balls or oval-shaped koftas and arrange on a tray.

Heat a wide frying pan (skillet) with some vegetable oil over a medium heat, and fry the koftas in batches for 5–6 minutes, turning them, until they are a nice golden colour all over. Remove from the pan to set aside and continue frying the rest of the koftas.

Heat the tomato sauce in wide, deep pan until it is almost boiling, then add the koftas to the sauce. Cover and cook over a medium heat for 30–35 minutes.

Serve with steamed basmati rice or in a pita with some tahini, if you like.

CHAPTER 6

HERBS

I use a lot of herbs in my cooking – in fact, I prefer to use fresh herbs over spices, as to me they act as an incredible enhancer to great ingredients, and are so versatile. I love coriander, parsley, chervil, fennel and chives, because often you can use the whole plant in different ways within one dish.

GREEN ZHOUG

Makes 300 g (10½ oz)

150 g (5½ oz) coriander
    (cilantro), coarsely
    chopped and most
    of the stalks discarded
10 fresh green chillies,
    coarsely chopped
5 garlic cloves, coarsely
    chopped
150 ml (5 fl oz/⅔ cup)
    vegetable oil
1 teaspoon ground coriander
¼ teaspoon sea salt

Zhoug is a Yemenite spicy condiment: it's almost like a salsa verde, but without the capers or anchovies. This is my version, which differs a little from a traditional zhoug, and it's a bit more accessible and easier to make. The fresh coriander (cilantro) and ground coriander combine to make a zingy sauce that works with almost anything. It's great with roasted vegetables, and delicious on a hummus plate. At the restaurant, we serve it with pork belly. Try it and see what you like to pair it with.

Place the coriander, chillies and garlic in a food processor and blitz for 2 minutes to get a smooth consistency yet with a bit of texture. Transfer to a bowl and gradually mix in the oil, ground coriander and salt. Store in a sealed container in the refrigerator where it will keep for up to 1 week.

IRAQI GREEN TORTILLA
WITH LEMON AND TAHINI

Serves 3–4

2 tablespoons olive oil
1 large onion, finely diced
1 green chilli, thinly sliced
100 g (3½ oz) coriander
    (cilantro), finely chopped
    and discard the stalks
100 g (3½ oz) flat-leaf
    parsley, finely chopped
    and discard the stalks
50 g (1¾ oz) mint, finely
    chopped and stalks
    discarded
30 g (1 oz) spring onions
    (scallions), finely sliced
6 large eggs
½ teaspoon ground cumin
1½ teaspoons sea salt

To serve
1 lemon, cut into wedges
Classic Tahini (page 60)
    or shop-bought
Chopped Salad (page 170)
    (optional)

Originated in Iraq, 'eeja' can also be found in the Iranian cuisine, where it is also known as 'kuku sabzi'. My version is more similar to the Spanish tortilla as I don't use any flour in the recipe. Don't be put off by the quantity of herbs that are going in here: it all comes together really well. I love to serve this with tahini and lemon to create a very herby and fresh flavour. Any leftovers would work brilliantly in a sandwich.

Preheat the oven to 180°C (350°F/gas 4).

Heat the oil in a frying pan (skillet) over a medium heat. Add the diced onion and green chilli and fry for 6–8 minutes until the onion is caramelised.

Place the chopped herbs and sliced spring onions in a bowl. Crack the eggs into the same bowl. Add the caramelised onions, chilli, ground cumin and salt, and whisk everything together.

Heat the olive oil in an ovenproof 26 cm (10 in) non-stick frying pan (skillet) over a medium-low heat. Let the pan heat up for 2 minutes then pour in the green egg mixture. Cook for 4–5 minutes then transfer to the oven and cook for a further 15 minutes. Remove from the oven and slide the tortilla onto a serving dish. Cut into portions and serve with lemon wedges, tahini and some chopped salad (optional).

FRESH HERB SALAD WITH CHERRIES AND ALMONDS

Serves 2

14 cherries, stones removed

30 g (1 oz) coriander (cilantro), coarsely chopped and leaves discarded

30 g (1 oz) flat-leaf parsley, coarsely chopped and stalks discarded

15 g (½ oz) spring onions (scallions), thinly sliced

50 g (1¾ oz) raw blanched almonds, coarsely chopped

1 mild green chilli, thinly sliced

4 tablespoons extra-virgin olive oil

2 tablespoons lemon juice

sea salt

This dish is like summer to me: I find it so refreshing and delicious. We started serving it at the restaurant last year and it has proved really popular. Try to find very sweet, firm cherries – not the soft type. The contrast between the sweet cherries and the spicy chillies is delicious, while the herbs add a fresh flavour that ties it all together. I like to serve this interesting dish as a starter. This recipe a take-off on Hila Alpert's iconic salad from the Basta in Tel Aviv.

Toss all the ingredients together in a mixing bowl. Season with salt to taste, and serve.

OREN

HERBS

RAW COURGETTE SALAD WITH MINT, BASIL AND TOASTED ALMONDS

Serves 2

1 large yellow courgette
(zucchini), trimmed
1 large green courgette
(zucchini), trimmed
30 g (1 oz) basil leaves,
chopped and stems
discarded
30 g (1 oz) mint leaves,
chopped and stems
discarded
20 ml (¾ fl oz) extra-virgin
olive oil
juice of ½ lemon
50 g (1¾ oz) flaked almonds,
toasted
sea salt and freshly ground
black pepper

I actually prefer courgette (zucchini) raw rather than cooked, and this salad is a great way to try it this way if you haven't before. Choose a lighter green courgette rather than one of the very dark ones: it will macerate beautifully in the dressing. Slicing the courgette thinly is important here, but don't go too thin, as you want to retain a bit of bite. Herby, fresh flavours are exactly what courgette needs, so the mint and basil make the perfect pairing, while the toasted almonds add a delicious crunch.

Slice the courgettes into 1 mm-thick strips using a mandoline. Place in a bowl with the herbs, olive oil, lemon juice and almonds, and season with salt and pepper. Toss gently with your hands so that you don't break the courgette strips. Serve immediately.

KOHLRABI WITH FRESH HERBS, CHILLI FLAKES AND TOASTED SOURDOUGH

Serves 2

4–5 tablespoons olive oil

1 garlic clove, bashed

2 slices of stale good-quality white sourdough, torn into 5 mm (¼ in) chunks

sea salt

juice of ½ lemon

2 large kohlrabi, peeled

30 g (1 oz) picked chervil leaves, chopped and stems discarded

3 spring onions (scallions), sliced

15 g (½ oz) picked coriander (cilantro) leaves, chopped and stems discarded

2 teaspoons sweet pul biber (or dried chilli flakes)

freshly ground black pepper

Like the Shaved Fennel (page 150) and the Raw Courgette Salad (page 136), this dish takes a vegetable that is usually cooked and presents it raw, allowing the full flavour to be enjoyed. As with the fennel and courgette, it's important for the kohlrabi to be thinly sliced and prepared with care to ensure the best possible texture for a salad.

The key thing is to make sure the kohlrabi is fresh – if you cut into a kohlrabi and it's dry inside, it's too old and won't taste good. You want it to have some moisture. This dish has a little hint of spice from chilli flakes, which works well. I like to serve it as part of a selection of small plates or as a starter rather than as a side dish, as it's quite robust.

Heat 2 tablespoons of olive oil and the garlic clove in a frying pan (skillet) over a medium heat. Add the chunks of sourdough and a pinch of salt and fry for 6–7 minutes until golden brown. Squeeze over the lemon juice and set aside.

Cut the kohlrabi into julienne strips of ½ cm. Put into a mixing bowl with the remaining 2–3 tablespoons of olive oil and all the other ingredients, including most of the toasted sourdough. Toss gently with your hands and top with the remaining toasted sourdough.

GREEN FALAFEL WITH TAHINI

Serves 4–6

600 g (1 lb 5 oz) dried
   chickpeas (garbanzos),
   soaked in plenty of water
   for 24 hours
1 white onion, coarsely
   chopped
15 g (½ oz) mild red chilli,
   coarsely chopped
4 garlic cloves, coarsely
   chopped
120 g (4 oz) coriander
   (cilantro) leaves, coarsely
   chopped
120 g (4 oz) flat-leaf parsley
   leaves, coarsely chopped
15 g (½ oz) ground cumin
10 g (¼ oz) ground coriander
10 g (¼ oz) white sesame
   seeds
½ teaspoon bicarbonate
   of soda
75 ml (2½ fl oz/⅓ cup)
   cold water
15 g (½ oz) sea salt
500 ml (17 fl oz/generous
   2 cups) vegetable oil,
   for frying
Classic Tahini (page 60)
   or shop-bought, to serve

I never used to like falafel all that much when I was growing up, but when I moved to the UK, it ended up being the first food from home that I missed, and I appreciate it so much more now. Here, I've used plenty of herbs to add flavour and give these falafels their green colour. It's important not to overcook them – you want the outsides to be crisp, but the insides to be moist. So, make sure the oil is really hot, and don't overcrowd the pan. That way, they'll cook quickly and taste delicious. Fry them right before serving: you don't want them sitting around.

Drain and rinse the chickpeas. Mix the chopped onion, chilli, garlic and the fresh herbs in a bowl with the chickpeas. Using a meat mincer with a fine attachment, start passing the mixture through the grinder into a bowl. Once everything is minced, add the spices, sesame seeds, bicarbonate of soda, salt and the water. Mix well with your fingers, then store in the refrigerator for 2–3 hours before frying.

Once the falafel mixture has firmed up, then it is ready to begin rolling. Roll the falafel into small balls about 4 cm (1½ in) in diameter.

Heat the oil in a deep pan to 175°C (350°F). Pan-fry a small quantity of the mixture to check the seasoning, and make any adjustments as necessary. Fry the falafel in batches (the oil will cool down if you add too many) and fry for 3–4 minutes, until golden brown. Drain on a paper towel or in a colander. Eat warm and serve with tahini.

GRILLED POTATOES WITH CORIANDER, LEMON AND GARLIC

Serves 4 as a side

500 g (1 lb 2 oz) baby
    potatoes
2 tablespoons extra-virgin
    olive oil
juice of ½ lemon
2 garlic cloves, coarsely
    chopped
15 g (½ oz) coriander
    (cilantro) leaves, chopped
sea salt

This dish is inspired by a restaurant in Tel Aviv that sells Bukharian food. Alongside their meat dishes, they serve homemade chips tossed in coriander (cilantro), lemon and garlic. They taste great, so here I've done something similar with Charlotte potatoes, which are boiled then hand-crushed before being roasted in olive oil, grilled over charcoal and tossed in the flavourings. I'm giving away a big secret with this recipe, as they're a huge favourite at the restaurant.

Preheat a charcoal grill or heat a griddle pan over a high heat.

Boil the potatoes in a pan of salted water for 20–25 minutes until tender to the point of a knife but not mushy. Drain, then – once they are cool enough to handle – crush the potatoes with your hands slightly: this will help give them a crunchy texture after grilling.

Grill the potatoes for 20–25 minutes until slightly charred.

Toss the grilled potatoes in a mixing bowl with the olive oil, lemon juice, garlic, coriander and a generous pinch of sea salt.

CAESAR SALAD WITH CURED SARDINES AND LABEN KISHK

Serves 2

15 leaves romaine or cos
　　lettuce hearts (the
　　white part)
handful of toasted
　　sourdough (page 140)
laben kishk or aged ricotta
　　salata, for grating

For the Caesar dressing
75 g (2¾ oz/4 large) egg yolks
175 ml (6 fl oz/¾ cup)
　　vegetable oil
20 g (¾ oz) Cured Sardines
　　(page 192)
1 large garlic clove, finely
　　grated
25 g (1 oz) lemon juice
1 tablespoon water
generous pinch of sea salt
　　and freshly ground black
　　pepper

Caesar salad is one of my favourite dishes. Here, I've created my own version using our cured sardines (page 192) instead of anchovies, and laben kishk in place of Parmesan. This dish is really popular at the restaurant, and has strong, bold flavours that complement each other perfectly.

To make the Caesar dressing, whisk the egg yolks in the bowl of a stand mixer fitted with the whisk attachment (or in a bowl with a handheld whisk) for about 2 minutes. Slowly start dripping the oil into the egg yolks then drizzle in a steady, thin stream of the oil, until totally emulsified. Purée the sardines using a pestle and mortar, then add them to the mixture (emulsified). Continue whisking slowly, adding the garlic, lemon juice, water and salt and pepper.

Wash the salad leaves in a bowl of iced water and leave for 10 minutes, then drain and spin dry in a salad spinner or pat dry gently with paper towel.

Place the leaves in a large mixing bowl. Add 3 tablespoons of the Caesar dressing and toss gently with your hands, making sure every leaf is covered with the dressing. Or lightly dip each salad leaf in the dressing, making sure they are well coated. Place on serving plates, add the toasted sourdough and grate lots of laben kishk on top.

CHAPTER 7

SALADS & GREENS

Where I come from, dishes that are predominately comprised of vegetables are common; it's just part of my culinary heritage that vegetables are more often the stars of the show than animal proteins. When putting together a meal, vegetables are present in many forms – hot, cold, raw, fried – and a lot of my recipes are heavy with a citrussy tang to give sharp contrast to the accompanying dishes on the table.

SHAVED FENNEL WITH LEMON, OLIVE OIL AND BARREL-AGED FETA

Serves 2

2 fennel bulbs, washed
   and halved lengthwise
30 g (1 oz) coriander
   (cilantro) leaves, picked
½ red onion, thinly sliced
20 ml (¾ fl oz) olive oil
juice of ½ lemon
sea salt and freshly ground
   black pepper
100 g (3½ oz) barrel-aged
   feta

I love fennel because it is a very versatile vegetable. If you're serving it raw, it's best to shave it into very thin slices using mandoline. When it is fresh it has a lovely anise note, but when roasted it delivers more depth of flavour and becomes wonderfully caramelised.

If you slice the fennel a little in advance, you can leave it to soften and marinate in the lemon juice, then just finish the dish with the remaining ingredients when you're ready to serve. I love the anise flavour of this salad: it pairs beautifully with fish for a fresh, summery dish. A really good barrel-aged feta is important here to balance the flavours.

Thinly shave the fennel using a mandoline. Place in a mixing bowl with the coriander and red onion, add the olive oil and lemon juice and season with salt and pepper. Toss gently with your hands. Crumble the feta over the top and serve.

GREEN BEAN SALAD WITH TOMATO PULP AND CHILLI

Serves 4

500 g (1 lb 2 oz) French
    beans, washed, trimmed
    and thinly sliced
2 shallots, diced
30 g (1 oz) oregano leaves,
    picked
juice of 1 lemon
1 red chilli, deseeded
    and diced
2 tablespoons extra-virgin
    olive oil
sea salt
5 salad tomatoes
freshly ground black pepper

I've used raw vegetables in this recipe that you might be used to seeing cooked – it's a great way to enjoy those green, fresh flavours that tend to get a bit lost when heated. The secret is to chop the beans very finely, almost spring onion (scallion)-style. The seasoning here is simple but robust, which makes it a great side for almost any dish. I like to serve this salad with bluefin tuna sashimi, and as it works really well with raw fish flavours, but feel free to experiment and find your own pairings.

Place the beans in a mixing bowl, add the shallots, oregano, lemon juice, diced chilli and olive oil. Season with salt. Quarter the tomatoes and scoop out the seeds, keeping the pulp whole. Arrange the bean salad on a plate and dollop the tomato pulp around the plate. Season with freshly ground black pepper. Eat with a spoon.

משלוחים ת
-6744479
שוק העליה
2 90
שוק העליה
2 90
שוק העליה
2 90
שוק העליה
2 90
4 90
4 90

SMOKED AUBERGINE WITH OLIVE OIL, SHALLOTS AND BASIL

Serves 3–4 as a starter (appetiser)

2 aubergines (eggplants)
3 tablespoons extra-virgin
   olive oil
1 tablespoons lemon juice
sea salt and freshly ground
   black pepper
2 tablespoons finely diced
   shallots
few picked basil leaves

Aubergines (eggplants) are one of my favourite vegetables, and the very best way to prepare them is to scorch them over an open flame, then peel away the burned skin: the smoky flavours infuse the flesh in a way that is just fantastic. You really do need an open flame to achieve this effect – you just don't get the same result any other way. Be patient, as this process takes some time. And don't be tempted to skip the draining step, as it's really key to get rid of any excess water before you season them.

When you're choosing aubergines, try to find ones that feel quite light in your hand – this means they'll contain less water and fewer seeds. And they don't like being kept in the refrigerator in any form. When you make this, serve it on the day and at room temperature.

Grill the aubergines over an open flame (either on a hob or barbecue) for 10–12 minutes, turning them continuously, until the aubergines are scorched on all sides and completely soft. Transfer the aubergines to a tray to cool slightly until you can handle them (the aubergines shouldn't cool down completely as then they'll be harder to peel). Peel off the charred skin, cut off the stems and place on a rack or a colander until most of the liquid has drained away. Cut the aubergines in half lengthwise and then into 4 cm (1½ in) chunks. Transfer with a spatula to a serving dish. Drizzle with plenty of olive oil and lemon juice, and season with salt and pepper. Sprinkle with the shallots and basil.

ROASTED BEETROOTS WITH SHERRY VINEGAR AND CHIVES

Serves 4

3 large golden beetroots
(beets), washed thoroughly
3 large red beetroots (beets),
washed thoroughly
3 tablespoons olive oil
sea salt and freshly ground
black pepper
2 tablespoons Jerez (sherry)
vinegar
4 tablespoons chives, finely
chopped, to serve

Here, we are roasting the beetroot (beets) until heavily charred. This adds so much flavour, as they will caramelise deliciously, but it does take time. You'll need to give them about an hour on a very high heat, but it might take even longer, depending on the size, so keep an eye on them. It's okay if you can't get golden beetroots, but do try and get really fresh ones – you want them to be firm rather than soft, ideally with the leaves, as that is a good indicator of their freshness. In the restaurant, I like to top this with some big chunks of feta, roasting it a final time before serving, to turn the feta golden and add a decadent touch.

Preheat the oven to its maximum temperature (roughly 240°C/430°F/Gas 9).

Pat the beetroots dry and place on a roasting tray (pan). Drizzle with 1 tablespoon of olive oil and season with salt and pepper. Roast in the oven for about 1 hour, or until the beetroots are slightly burnt and tender but not entirely soft. Remove from the oven and leave the beetroots to cool slightly, before peeling the away the skins with your hands. Cut each peeled beetroot into 6 or 8 wedges, depending on their size.

Season the beetroot wedges with salt and pepper, dress with the sherry vinegar and the remaining olive oil, and sprinkle the chives on top.

GRILLED HISPI CABBAGE AND ROMESCO

Serves 4 as a side or starter

1 hispi cabbage
sea salt and freshly ground
   black pepper
500 ml (17 fl oz/generous
   2 cups) vegetable stock
   (page 80)

For the romesco
300 g (10½ oz) (about 3–4)
   romano peppers
35 g (1¼ oz) confit garlic
   (page 90)
30 g (1 oz) toasted blanched
   almonds
25 ml (¾ fl oz) olive oil
5 g (¼ fl oz) salt
pinch of sweet and smoked
   paprika
pinch of crushed black
   pepper
2 teaspoons Jerez (sherry)
   vinegar

This is one of the most popular dishes in the restaurant, and we've been serving it from day one, whenever hispi cabbages are in season. People favour it over meat and fish dishes as it's got so much interest and flavour. Hispi has a sweeter taste, and it doesn't take long to cook. We cook this over a charcoal grill, and it's important to go to this effort in order to get the best results.

Preheat the oven to 200°C (400°F/gas 6) and prepare a charcoal grill.

To make the romesco, start by roasting the peppers over an open flame (either on the hob or barbecue) until they are burnt all over. Leave them to cool slightly, before peeling them by hand and deseeding them. Then place all the ingredients in a food processor and pulse to a semi coarse consistency. Set aside.

Cut the hispi in half lengthwise. Season with salt and pepper and place cut-side down in a roasting tray (pan). Pour in the vegetable stock and roast in the oven for 15–20 minutes, until just soft. Remove from the stock, which can now be discarded, and let drain. Grill over charcoal for 5–7 minutes until blackened all over. Serve with a dollop of romesco on top.

SCORCHED OKRA WITH OLIVE OIL, FRESH TOMATOES AND LABEN KISHK

Serves 2

5–6 extra-virgin olive oil
250 g (9 oz) okra, washed,
   dried and cut into 1 cm
   (½ in)-thick rings
2 sivri pepper (mild Turkish
   pepper), chopped
1 red onion, coarsely diced
1 large tomato, diced
5 sage leaves, thinly sliced
2 garlic cloves, sliced
juice of 1 lemon
10 g (¼ oz) laben kishk
   or aged ricotta salata,
   for grating
15 picked mint leaves,
   roughly chopped

The key to delicious okra is to cook it quickly, at a high temperature, so you don't overcook it. We use a very hot griddle, but you can use a cast-iron pan (skillet). Just make sure you get it really hot before you add the okra. Flash-frying the okra in this way means is still has plenty of bite. Laben kishk is a fermented dried yoghurt, but if you can't get hold of it, try ricotta salata instead. Choose the smallest okra you can, as they will have the nicest texture.

Heat a cast-iron frying pan (skillet) or a plancha over a high heat with 2 tablespoons of olive oil. Once the skillet is smoking, add the sliced okra and chillies. Leave for 1–2 minutes until they are lightly charred, then stir-fry for another 1–2 minutes. Add the onion, tomatoes, sage and garlic and cook for another 3–4 minutes. Finish with the remaining 3–4 tablespoons of olive oil, lemon juice, salt and mint. Grate plenty of laben kishk on top. Serve hot.

GRILLED SWEETCORN, FRESH PEAS AND BARREL-AGED FETA

Serves 2

2 fresh corn on the cob
(husks intact)
500 g (1 lb) peas,
freshly podded
½ red onion, diced
20 ml (¾ fl oz) extra-virgin
olive oil
juice of ½ lemon
2 tablespoons picked
oregano leaves
100 g (3½ oz) barrel-aged feta
sea salt and freshly ground
black pepper

The crunchy smokiness of the corn, the full green flavour of the peas, and the creamy, tangy feta is just delicious. Make this in the summer when the ingredients are at their best.

Preheat a charcoal grill.

Grill the corn on the hot grill for 15 minutes, turning the corn so they blacken evenly. Carefully remove the husks then continue grilling the corn without the husk for 3–4 minutes, turning the cobs so they brown evenly. Remove from the grill and let the corn cool down, then remove the kernels from the cob with a sharp knife.

Prepare a bowl of iced water. Cook the peas in a pan of salted boiling water for 2 minutes, then drain and transfer to the iced water. Drain the peas from the iced water, then warm through in a sauté pan with the corn for 3–4 minutes with a little oil.

Once the peas and corn are hot, transfer to a mixing bowl and add the onion, olive oil, lemon juice and oregano, and season with salt and pepper. Crumble the feta over the dish and serve warm.

BUTTER LETTUCE WITH SEASONAL VEGETABLES AND ZA'ATAR

Serves 4

2 whole butter (bibb) lettuce, stem removed and outer leaves discarded

2 mini cucumbers (7–8 cm/ 2¾–3¼ in long), cut into large 4 cm (1½ in) chunks

4 plum tomatoes, cut into large 4 cm (1½ in) chunks

1 sweet red (bell) pepper, deseeded and cut into large 4 cm (1½ in) chunks

½ red onion, coarsely diced

2 tablespoons lemon juice

4 tablespoons extra-virgin olive oil

sea salt and freshly ground black pepper

1 tablespoon Za'atar (page 18)

This all-season fresh salad is great as part of a brunch spread, as it pairs really well with a quiche or eggs. Use the best cucumbers, tomatoes and pepper you can find – this is one of those recipes where you really want to let the ingredients speak for themselves. The za'atar adds interest and gives it a slightly different kick – citrussy and tangy.

Place the white leaves of the butter lettuce in a bowl of iced water for 10 minutes, then remove and dry in a salad spinner or pat dry gently with paper towel.

Place the cubed vegetables in a mixing bowl. Add the lettuce. Add the lemon juice and olive oil, season with salt and pepper, and toss gently. Sprinkle with the za'atar and serve.

CHOPPED SALAD

Serves 2

5 good-quality, ripe
tomatoes, cut into 2–3 mm
(1/16–1/8 in) dice
3 mini cucumbers (Turkish
or Greek style), cut into
2–3 mm (1/16–1/8 in) dice
½ white onion, cut into
2–3 mm (1/16–1/8 in) dice
30 g (1 oz) flat-leaf
parsley, chopped and
stalks discarded
15 g (½ oz) mint, chopped
and stalks discarded
25 ml (¾ fl oz) extra-virgin
olive oil
25 ml (¾ fl oz) lemon juice
sea salt and freshly ground
black pepper
100 g (3½ oz) Classic Tahini
(page 60) or shop-bought,
to serve

You'll find this dish almost everywhere in Israel. Some places call it Israeli salad, some call it Arab salad – I just call it chopped salad. As a kid, I used to love going to restaurants with my dad. We'd sit at the bar and watch the chefs chopping the fresh ingredients for this salad right in front of us, and I used to dream of opening a place devoted to a truly delicious chopped salad prepared freshly in front of customers. As ever, get the best tomatoes and cucumbers you can find – you don't want to make this dish with hard-skinned cucumbers that taste watery and bland. Seasoning is key, as is straining the tomatoes before you add them to the salad. This really is an all-day dish – I enjoy it for breakfast with a boiled egg and tahini, then have it on the table at lunch or dinner as part of a spread of other vegetable and meat dishes. It pairs deliciously with fish, but could also be a meal in itself.

Place the diced tomatoes in a sieve or colander to drain the excess water. Combine everything in a mixing bowl and season with salt and pepper. Mix gently with a spoon. Pile into a bowl and serve with the tahini on the top.

CHAPTER 8

GRAINS, LEGUMES & PULSES

Grains and pulses are on the table at every meal; lentils, cracked wheat, butter beans, wild rice, freekeh and chickpeas are so much a part of the cuisine. If there are ten to twelve dishes on a table, then at least four of them will include grains. And this isn't just at home – they are served in restaurants and as part of street-food dishes, too. Here, I've included some of my favourite ways to cook them.

BAKED BUTTER BEANS WITH BARREL-AGED FETA AND SLOW-ROAST TOMATOES

Serves 8 as a starter or side

500 g (1 lb 2 oz) dried butter
    (lima) beans, soaked in
    plenty of water for 24 hours
200 ml (7 fl oz/scant 1 cup) dry
    white wine
8 garlic cloves
1 teaspoon sea salt
½ teaspoon freshly ground
    black pepper
10 g (¼ oz) thyme sprigs
2 bay leaves
Slow-roast Tomatoes
    (page 80)
200 g (7 oz) barrel-aged feta
25 ml (¾ fl oz) olive oil

Baking the beans in white wine, garlic and herbs results in rich, tasty juices, while the grilled feta topping adds a tangy, indulgent finish. It's important to use a generous amount of really good feta here. At the restaurant, we serve it in individual dishes, but you can make it in a big dish and place it in the middle of the table along with some crusty sourdough bread so that everyone can dive in.

Preheat the oven to 180°C (350°F/gas 4).

Drain and rinse the butter beans and place them in a deep roasting tray (pan). Add the rest of the ingredients, except the feta and olive oil, to the tray and mix well with your hands. Add enough water so that the beans are submerged – the water level needs to sit about 2 cm (¾ in) above the beans. Cover the tray with aluminium foil and seal tightly. Bake in the oven for 2–3 hours, until the beans are thoroughly cooked and half of the liquid has been absorbed by the beans. If a lot of liquid remains, then transfer the beans to a stockpot and reduce over a medium heat by half. Preheat the oven grill. Crumble the feta over the beans, drizzle the beans with the olive oil and place under the hot grill until the cheese has turned golden. Serve straight from the oven.

FUL MEDAMES – SLOW-COOKED BROAD BEANS WITH LEMON, CHILLI AND TAHINI

Serves 5–6

500 g (1 lb 2 oz) dried broad
    (fava) beans, soaked in
    plenty of water for 24 hours
25 ml (¾ oz) olive oil, plus
    extra for drizzling
5 garlic cloves, peeled
100 g (3½ oz) Classic Tahini
    (page 60) or shop-bought
1 tablespoon lemon juice
sea salt

For the chilli paste

5 green mild chillies
2 garlic cloves
2 tablespoons lemon juice

To serve

1 tablespoon finely chopped
    white onions per person
1 tablespoon chopped
    flat-leaf parsley

This is a classic Egyptian dish. Served warm, it's made up of split broad (fava) beans, slow-cooked with spices until they're very soft and almost entirely broken down – the final texture is creamy. The ratio of liquid to beans is important, so you need to keep an eye on the beans as they cook and make sure that the mixture doesn't dry out. Top with tahini and lemon to finish and serve with a pita. In Tel Aviv, you would find ful served as a breakfast food alongside hummus, and it does make a great brunch option topped with an egg.

Start by making the chilli paste, by putting the ingredients in a food processor and blending until they are a coarse paste.

Drain the beans and rinse well. Place in a large stockpot and fill with water until the water level sits 3 cm (1¼ in) above the beans. Add the olive oil and garlic, bring to the boil, then reduce the heat and simmer for about 2 hours, or until the beans are completely falling apart. The beans should almost be a paste-like consistency so you might need to add a bit more water to reach this consistency. Once the beans are nice and creamy, scoop 2 large spoonfuls of the ful into a bowl. Top with a spoonful of tahini, plenty of olive oil and a little lemon juice. Season with salt to taste.

Serve with chopped onions and parsley on the side.

MEJADRA WITH WILD RICE, SPECKLED LENTILS AND TAHINI YOGHURT

Serves 4–6 as a side

vegetable oil
150 g (5½ oz/¾ cup)
   basmati rice
75 g (2¾ oz/⅓ cup) wild rice
150 g (5½ oz) beluga lentils
   or Puy lentils
1 garlic clove, peeled
sea salt and freshly ground
   black pepper
500 g (1 lb 2 oz) finely
   diced onions (weight after
   they have been peeled)
½ teaspoon ground cinnamon
pinch of ground cumin
100 g (3½ oz) Greek yoghurt
100 g (3½ oz) Classic Tahini
   (page 60) or shop-bought

To serve

150 g (5½ oz) toasted
   almonds flakes
7 spring onions (scallions),
   finely sliced

This is a classic Arab dish and a favourite recipe of mine. I've spent years playing around with the components, arriving at something that differs slightly from the traditional approach of cooking it all together: here, everything is cooked separately which helps to achieve a good result. Be sure to use a good-quality long-grain rice that isn't going to fall apart. Mejadra is great on its own, but I like to serve it with yoghurt and tahini. The onions are a key element here – cooked slowly until really brown and sweetly caramelised, they bring the dish together, while the toasted flaked almonds add a crunchy finish.

Heat 1 tablespoon of oil in a heavy-based saucepan over a medium heat, add the basmati rice and fry for 2 minutes. The ratio of rice to boiling water that is needed is 1:1.5. Therefore, once the rice is weighed, pour it into a mug to measure its volume, measure one and half parts of boiling water to the saucepan (about 225 ml/7½ fl oz) and a generous pinch of salt. Reduce the heat to low, cover the pan tightly with a lid and cook for 14 minutes. Remove from the heat and keep the lid on for 5 minutes, then remove the lid and fluff the rice gently with a wooden spoon. Set aside to cool down.

Cook the wild rice in plenty of boiling water as if you're cooking pasta for 25–35 minutes. The rice is cooked when it's soft and it has split. Drain and set aside.

Place the lentils in a saucepan and cover with cold water. Add the garlic clove and a pinch of salt and pepper, and cook for about 25 minutes until tender but still firm.

Heat 5 tablespoons of oil in a heavy-based saucepan over a medium heat, add the onions and cook for about 20 minutes until all the liquid has evaporated and the onions have turned golden brown and caramelised.

Preheat the oven to 180°C (350°F/Gas 4).

Mix the basmati rice, wild rice, lentils, onions, spices and almonds very gently with your hands in a bowl (you want to avoid the rice breaking). Transfer to a deep oven tray (pan), cover with aluminium foil and reheat in the oven for about 20 minutes.

Combine the Greek yoghurt and tahini in a bowl. Pile the mejadra on a plate and spoon some of the tahini-yoghurt mixture on the top. Scatter with the almonds and spring onions.

CHOLENT – SLOW-COOKED STEW OF GRAINS AND BEEF

Serves 4–6

8 medium potatoes, peeled (Desiree, ideally)
4 onions, peeled
2 garlic bulbs, halved widthways
150 g (5½ oz) dried butter (lima) beans, soaked overnight in plenty of water
150 g (5½ oz) dried kidney beans
2 kg (4 lb 8 oz) beef chuck, cut into 5–6 cm (2–2½ in) chunks
500 g (1 lb 2 oz) bone marrow
200 g (7 oz) beef short ribs
5 bay leaves
6 eggs
1 tablespoon sea salt
½ tablespoon freshly ground black pepper
150 g (5½ oz) whole dried barley, soaked overnight in plenty of water
House Pickles (page 24), to serve

This is a traditional Jewish Ashkenazi dish that I used to have as a kid. This is home-style cooking at its best. It's traditional to serve on Shabbat: as it's a day of rest, you're not allowed to cook, but this stew can be prepared before the day of rest begins, then left to simmer over a low heat, ready to enjoy when you return from the synagogue. This isn't how I think of it, though. To me, it's simply a comforting, homely dish that my grandma on my father's side used to make. She would cook it over a very low kerosene stove for 12 hours, filling the whole house with the aromas of the beans and meat cooking. This is one of those dishes with dozens of variations, and you'll see it prepared differently in many different countries: there's a Moroccan way, a European way, and so on. To me, it's home. You will need at least 12 hours to cook the cholent, plus soaking the barley the night before.

Preheat the oven to 125°C (250°F/gas ¼).

Start by placing the whole potatoes in the bottom of a large casserole dish or ovenproof lidded pan. Follow with the whole onions and the garlic. For the next layer, put the butter beans on one half of the pan and the kidney beans in another half of the pan. The next layer is the meat: spread the beef chuck and the bone marrow out evenly over the beans and grains. Put the bay leaves and the eggs on top. Cover with enough water so it comes up 3 cm (1¼ in) above the last layer and add plenty of salt and black pepper. Place the pan on the hob and bring to the boil, then cover with a lid and transfer to the oven. Bake for 6 hours.

Wrap the barley in a piece of muslin cloth but not tightly – you need to leave room for it to expand at least twice in volume – and place in the pan. Transfer back into the oven and bake for another 6 hours.

The cholent is ready when all the liquid has evaporated. Remove the muslin cloth parcel and transfer everything to a large serving tray. Keep the eggs unpeeled for everyone to peel their own, and serve with pickles.

WARM FREEKEH SALAD WITH LABEN KISHK AND PINE NUTS

Serves 4

130 g (4½ oz) freekeh wheat,
  rinsed and drained
2 garlic cloves, slightly
  crushed
2 oregano sprigs
sea salt and freshly ground
  black pepper
25 ml (¾ oz) olive oil
juice of ½ lemon
30 g (1 oz) flat-leaf parsley,
  finely sliced with stems
  discarded
30 g (1 oz) chopped
  coriander (cilantro), finely
  sliced and stems discarded
2 large spring onions
  (scallions), finely sliced
  and stems discarded
50 g (1¾ oz) toasted pine nuts
20 g (¾ oz) laben kishk
  or aged ricotta salata

Freekeh is a roasted green wheat with a lovely smoky flavour. It's really easy to pair with a whole range of other ingredients. You can even make risotto with freekeh instead of rice: it imparts a nutty, smoky taste. Here, I've used it in a bold, hearty salad with garlic, lemon, fresh herbs and laben kishk, a fermented dried yoghurt. In Israel, we call it 'yoghurt stone', and I think of it as almost like the Middle-Eastern equivalent of Parmesan: it gives a rich umami flavour, salty and pungent. It can be tricky to get hold of, so if you can't get find it, you can use ricotta salata.

Put the freekeh, garlic and oregano in a stockpot and add some salt and pepper. Add enough water to sit 5 cm (2 in) above the freekeh, and cook over a medium heat for about 30 minutes until the freekeh is soft but not overcooked – it should still have a bit of bite. Drain the freekeh, removing the garlic and oregano, and transfer to a sauté pan. Warm the freekeh over a medium heat with some of the olive oil. Season again to taste with salt and pepper and sauté for 3–4 minutes. Remove from the heat, then remove and discard the crushed garlic cloves before adding the rest of the olive oil. Add the lemon juice, fresh herbs and toasted pine nuts. Grate plenty of laben kishk over the top.

CHAPTER 9

FISH & SEAFOOD

Fish is one of my favourite foods. Back home in Tel Aviv, we eat more fish than meat, which is pretty typical of the Mediterranean diet. I've had extensive experience of cooking fish and seafood in different restaurants, and it's such an interesting and varied ingredient. The recipes I've shared here are friendly and forgiving. Nobody is asking you to cook the perfect fillet; it's all about working with great ingredients and simple methods. There are a lot of recipes here compared to the other chapters, but in all honesty, I could have added even more.

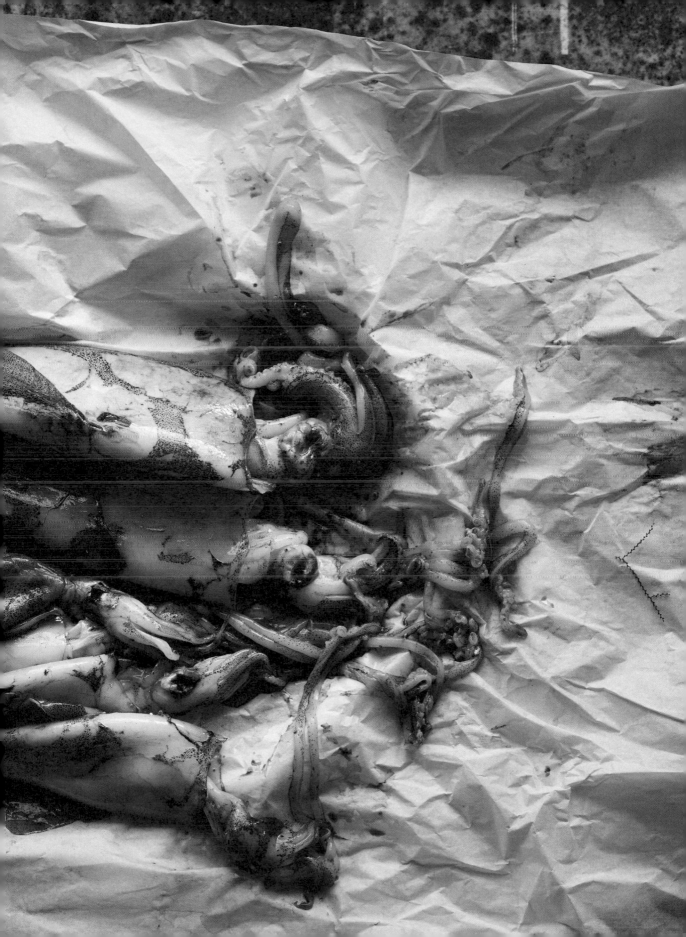

CURED SARDINES WITH OLIVE OIL AND LEMON ZEST

Serves 4–6 as a starter (appetiser)

500 g (1 lb 2 oz) whole
    sardines (ungutted)
1 kg (2 lb 4 oz) coarse salt
200 ml (7 fl oz/scant 1 cup)
    olive oil
2 bay leaves
5 allspice berries
grated zest of 1 lemon

Cured fish is a big part of the menu at Oren, and I always enjoy experimenting by pairing it with different flavours. Sardines aren't particularly easy to fillet, but the result is so rewarding; it really is worth it. You need to allow some time for this recipe, as the fish takes 24–48 hours to cure (depending on the size). The sardines are ready to go as soon as they're in the oil, but they'll keep for up to 3 weeks. They're great on their own, with a little of the infused oil drizzled over them to serve, but I also like to incorporate them in a lot of meals at my restaurant. One of my favourites is to make a Caesar salad with cured sardines instead of anchovies.

Place the sardines in a deep tray and cover completely with the salt. Leave the sardines to cure in the refrigerator for 24–48 hours, depending on their size. For sardines of about 50 g (1¾ oz), cure for 24 hours, and for 80 g (2¾ oz) plus, cure for 48 hours.

Remove the sardines from the salt and rinse with cold running water. Cut off all the heads. Using a paring knife, cut a split of about 1 cm (½ in) in the belly of each sardine and remove the insides while holding the sardine under cold running water. Put both your thumbs into the now-cleaned belly and push down until you feel the spine with your thumbs and separate it from the flesh – repeat with all the sardines. You will have butterflied the sardines. Both sides of each sardine will have two fillets, which are separated by a blood line. Remove all four fillets from each sardine and place in a container. Cover with the olive oil, add the bay leaves and allspice berries and cover. The sardines can be kept in the refrigerator for up 3 weeks, just make sure the fillets are submerged in the olive oil.

To serve, place the cured sardines on a plate with some of the olive oil and freshly grated lemon zest.

CRAB SALAD WITH AVOCADO, LAMB'S LETTUCE AND FRAGRANT HERBS

Serves 2

1 ripe avocado, halved,
    stoned, peeled and thinly
    sliced
sea salt
juice of ½ lemon
200 g (7 oz) picked white
    crab meat
80 g (2¾ oz) lamb's lettuce
    or corn salad
4 tablespoons chervil leaves
4 tablespoons coriander
    (cilantro) leaves
2 tablespoons picked
    mint leaves
2 tablespoons olive oil
freshly ground black pepper

This is a great winter salad when avocado is in season in Europe. The avocado needs to be just right – not overripe, not underripe – so it really is best to buy them in season. Avocado pairs really well with seafood flavours. If you can't get fresh crab meat, try this with lobster meat or prawns. The fresh herbs and leaves – chervil, mint, crunchy lamb's lettuce – are vital here. It's all about those vibrant, in-season flavours.

Fan out the avocado slices on a plate. Season with sea salt and lemon juice. Place all the remaining ingredients in a mixing bowl and toss gently with the olive oil, lemon juice, and some salt and pepper. To serve, place the salad on top of the avocado.

GRILLED OCTOPUS SALAD WITH JEREZ VINEGAR AND CHILLI

Serves 4–6 as a starter (appetiser)

2 bay leaves
1 fennel bulb, quartered
5 allspice berries
500 g (1 lb 2 oz) fresh
    and cleaned or frozen
    octopus (thawed if frozen)

For the salad
150 g (5½ oz) sweet red
    Romano peppers,
    deseeded and cut into
    3 x 0.5 cm (1¼ x ¼ in) strips
2 garlic cloves, thinly sliced
2 mild, red chilli, deseeded
    and thinly sliced into rings
1 small red onion, finely sliced
50 g (1¾ oz) coriander
    (cilantro) leaves, picked
    and coarsely chopped
2 tablespoons extra-virgin
    olive oil
4 tablespoons Jerez
    (sherry) vinegar
sea salt and freshly ground
    black pepper

Octopus is a very forgiving ingredient to work with, and you can use frozen or fresh for this recipe. Just don't overcook it – you want it to retain a little bite. Keep checking it as you cook; have a little taste and see if it's ready. You can make this salad a few hours in advance and keep it in the refrigerator – it will become even more delicious as the flavours mingle. It's almost like a cooked ceviche. It's really important to use a good vinegar here. I like to use Jerez, which is a sherry vinegar, but a Champagne vinegar would work well too. Just don't use malt! The fennel adds a nice aniseed flavour. Sometimes I like to add fennel to the stock too, but octopus are so full of flavour – that wonderful taste of the sea – that it's not essential. The leftover stock is great for a seafood risotto.

Put the bay leaves, quartered fennel and allspice in a large stockpot, fill the pot with cold water and place the octopus in it. Put a weighted plate on top of the octopus to prevent it from floating to the top and cook over a medium heat for 1½ hours. How long it takes to cook depends on the size and thickness of the octopus. The best way of finding out if it's fully cooked is by cutting off a small slice from one of the tentacles and tasting it. If it's still chewy, it needs more time. Once ready, drain the octopus and set aside to cool down.

Cut the octopus tentacles into 1 cm (½ in) rings. Place all the salad ingredients in a mixing bowl and toss with the olive oil and vinegar. Season with salt and pepper and serve at room temperature.

BRAISED CUTTLEFISH WITH SLOW-ROAST TOMATOES AND CHICKPEAS

Serves 4–6

**For the fish stock (makes
2 litres/68 fl oz/8½ cups stock)**
1 white onion, coarsely chopped
1 carrot, peeled and coarsely
    chopped
1 fennel bulb, coarsely chopped
2 bay leaves
5 allspice berries
1 kg (2 lb 4 oz) fish bones
    and heads
3 litres (102 fl oz/12¾ cups)
    cold water

For the chickpeas
250 g (9 oz) dried chickpeas
(garbanzos), soaked in plenty
    of water for 24 hours
½ teaspoon bicarbonate of soda

For the cuttlefish
30 ml (1 fl oz) olive oil
1 kg (2 lb 4 oz) cuttlefish, cleaned
    and cut into 3–4 cm (1¼–1½ in)
    long and 1 cm (½ in) wide strips
8 garlic cloves, sliced
1 red chilli, deseeded
    and thinly sliced
30 g (1 oz) oregano leaves
sea salt and freshly ground
    black pepper
juice of 1 lemon

To serve
3–4 quarters Slow-roasted
    Tomatoes (page 80)
    per serving
1 tablespoon chopped flat-leaf
    parsley per serving
generous drizzle of extra-virgin
    olive oil

This hearty, wintery seafood dish is almost like a stew. The flavour of cuttlefish is similar to squid, and when cooked properly – low and slow – it becomes really tender and the taste is out there. Cleaning it can be a task, I admit, but your fishmonger can do that for you. Searing the cuttlefish first is important, as it gives you a lovely brown, burnished fish, while the chickpeas (garbanzos) add a Mediterranean touch.

Tip: Adding bicarbonate of soda (baking soda) to the chickpeas helps to soften them, but only a little is needed.

To make the fish stock, put all the vegetables, bay leaves and allspice in a stockpot with the fish bones and cover with the cold water. Bring to the boil, then reduce the heat and simmer for 1½ hours, skimming the foam from the top regularly. Strain the stock. The stock can be kept in the refrigerator for up to 1 week, or in the freezer for up to 3 months.

To cook the chickpeas, drain and rinse them, then place in a saucepan and cover with cold water. Add the bicarbonate of soda, bring to the boil, then reduce the heat and simmer for about 1 hour. The chickpeas should be thoroughly cooked and tender but not mushy. Leave to cool in their cooking liquid while cooking the cuttlefish.

To cook the cuttlefish, heat the olive oil in a heavy-based saucepan (preferably cast-iron) over a medium heat then, when the oil gets smoky, add the cuttlefish strips and fry in batches for 5–6 minutes until nice and golden in colour. Add the sliced garlic and chilli. Add enough of the fish stock to cover the cuttlefish, then add the oregano, 1 teaspoon of salt and 1 teaspoon of ground pepper to the pan, cover the pan with a lid and cook for about 2 hours or until the cuttlefish is tender. Add the chickpeas right at the end. They only need about 3 minutes to be reheated. Season with lemon juice to taste.

Serve topped with slow-roasted tomatoes, chopped parsley and olive oil.

 OREN

HAKE ARAYES WITH LAMB FAT AND SPICED YOGHURT

Serves 4–6

3 pitas
600 g (1 lb 5 oz) Hake kebab
   mix (page 88)
50 g (1¾ oz) lamb fat
   (or duck fat)

For the spiced yoghurt
250 g (9 oz) thick goat
   or sheep's yoghurt
¼ teaspoon sumac
¼ teaspoon ground cumin
1 teaspoon lemon juice
sea salt

This is an Arabic dish. 'Arayes' roughly translates as 'bride', with the implication being that the meat is 'marrying' the pita. In the classic dish, the pitas are stuffed with spiced minced (ground) lamb, then grilled with the meat inside, but here I've used hake. It's quite a meaty fish, meaning it can stand up to this treatment well, but I have added a little lamb fat to impart some of the flavour and richness of the original. It is best to make this one over charcoal if you can, for that smoky street-food finish. I like to serve this as an informal starter (appetiser) – just dip the stuffed pitas into the spiced yoghurt and eat with your hands.

Preheat a charcoal grill or heat a griddle pan (skillet) over a high heat. If using the griddle pan, then preheat the oven to 190°C (375°F/gas 5).

Make a small slit with a sharp knife in the side of the pitas and fill the pitas with the hake kebab mix.

Mix all the spiced yoghurt ingredients in a bowl and store in the refrigerator until you're ready to serve.

When the grill is ready, brush the pitas with the lamb (or duck) fat on both sides and grill for 3–4 minutes on each side, until the fish is cooked through. If using a griddle pan, then finish cooking the pita in the oven for 8–10 minutes, or until the fish is cooked through.

Cut the pitas into quarters and serve hot with the spiced yoghurt for dipping.

BUTTERFLIED GRILLED MACKEREL WITH FRESH HERBS AND LEMON

Serves 2 as a starter (appetiser)

2 mackerel (about 350 g/
   12 oz each once butterflied)
25 g (1 oz) mint leaves,
   picked
25 g (1 oz) chervil leaves,
   picked
25 g (1 oz) flat-leaf parsley
   leaves, picked
25 g (1 oz) picked dill fronds
25 g (1 oz) Preserved Lemon
   (page 78), coarsely
   chopped
1 tablespoon olive oil
juice of ½ lemon
sea salt and freshly ground
   black pepper

I've given instructions here for cooking this on a charcoal grill, but it can be made in a frying pan (skillet) if you prefer. The key thing is to cook the fish on the skin side for 75 per cent of the cooking time, so that you get the skin nice and crispy before flipping it over to finish it off on the other side. Use the freshest mackerel you can get, as it really is the star of the show here. Mackerel is a fatty fish, so I've paired it with fresh herbs, salad and preserved lemon, all of which cut through the richness nicely.

Preheat a charcoal grill to a high heat.

Cut off all the heads. Using a paring knife, cut a split of about 1 cm (½ in) in the belly of each mackerel and remove the insides while holding the mackerel under cold running water. Put both your thumbs into the now-cleaned belly and push down until you feel the spine with your thumbs and separate it from the flesh – repeat with the other mackerel. You will have butterflied the mackerel.

Place the mackerel skin-side down on the hot grill and cook for 4 minutes, then flip the mackerel and grill the other side for 2 minutes. When ready, transfer to a plate. Toss the herbs with preserved lemon in a bowl, drizzle with the olive oil and lemon juice, and season with salt and pepper. Place the herb and lemon mix on top of the mackerel and enjoy.

BARBECUED LANGOUSTINES WITH BUTTER AND FRESH OREGANO

Serves 4 as a starter (appetiser)

4 large live langoustines

For the seasoned butter
100 g (3½ oz) good-quality
  unsalted butter
15 g (½ oz) picked oregano
  leaves
2 tablespoons lemon juice
2 garlic cloves, finely chopped
1 teaspoon sweet pul biber (or
  dried chilli flakes)

This is one of those recipes where a charcoal grill really is essential. When in season, langoustines are so sweet and delicious that you could enjoy them with just a drizzle of olive oil, but this seasoned butter, with lemon, garlic, pul biber and fresh oregano takes it to the next level.

Preheat a charcoal grill to a high heat.

To make the seasoned butter, put all the butter ingredients in a small saucepan and heat for 3–4 minutes to infuse the butter. Remove from the heat and set aside.

The easiest way to kill and cut the langoustine is to get a sharp kitchen knife and pierce the top of its head and pull the knife straight down onto its body. Remove the intestinal tract by scraping it with the back of a spoon. Cut right through the shell without completely cutting through to the other side, so you can open and butterfly the langoustine. Grill over hot coals, shell-side down, for about 4 minutes. Flip the langoustines onto its flesh and cook for about 2 more minutes. Remove the langoustines from the grill and transfer to a plate. Spoon over a couple of spoons of the seasoned butter and serve immediately.

MONKFISH IN LIBYAN CHRAIME SAUCE

Serves 2

2 x 200 g (7 oz) monkfish steaks
    (on the bone)
sea salt and freshly ground
    black pepper
Challah (page 100), to serve
    (optional)

**For the chraime sauce
(makes about 450 ml/15 fl oz/
scant 2 cups)**

2 tablespoons vegetable oil
4–5 garlic cloves, crushed
    (½ teaspoon once crushed)
100 g (3½ oz) tomato purée
    (paste)
pinch of hot chilli powder
10 g sweet paprika
5 g (¼ oz) ground cumin
10 g ground caraway seeds
pinch of sea salt
350 ml (12 fl oz/1½ cups) water
1 teaspoon lemon juice

Spicy chraime sauce (page 108) is a Libyan recipe that pairs perfectly with fish. It is usually served with larger fish, sliced into steaks on the bone as we've done here, as the gelatine in the bones further enriches the sauce. However, this isn't essential, and the sauce is also delicious with fillets if that's your preference. Here, I've given the same method we use in the restaurant: we grill the monkfish over charcoal and then serve it with the sauce, so that the smokiness of the fish imparts another layer of flavour. If you don't have a charcoal grill, though, you can simply poach the fish in the sauce for 8–10 minutes, or until it's pretty much falling off the bone, without grilling it first. It will still taste fantastic.

To make the chraime sauce, heat the oil in a heavy-based saucepan over a medium heat, add the garlic and cook for 2 minutes, then add tomato purée. Stir and cook for a further 3 minutes, then add all the spices and the salt while constantly stirring. Add the water, stir with a whisk, bring to the boil and simmer for 45 minutes. Add the lemon juice and remove from the heat.

Prepare a charcoal grill or heat a griddle pan over a high heat.

Season the monkfish steaks with salt and pepper. Grill the monkfish steaks for 4 minutes on each side, or until it flakes off the bone when touched. Reheat the chraime sauce. Place the fish in deep plates and pour the sauce over the fish. Serve with challah, if you would like.

SPICED CHOPPED POLLOCK
SALAD WITH SILKY TOMATOES

Serves 4

4 tablespoons olive oil
250 g (9 oz) pollock fillet
  (skin on)
sea salt
150 g (5½ oz) cucumber,
  finely diced
25 g (1 oz) shallot, diced
1 red chilli, deseeded
  and finely diced
50 g (1¾ oz) pine nuts, toasted
30 g (1 oz) coriander
  (cilantro) leaves, picked
1 tablespoon lemon juice
25 g (1 oz) Slow roast
  Tomatoes (page 80)
freshly ground black pepper

For the silky tomatoes
2 large ripe tomatoes
1 tablespoon olive oil

This is a bold chopped salad with robust flavours, and with the toasted pine nuts, fresh green herbs and silky-smooth tomatoes, plus that all-important crispy fish skin, it's a real textural feast. You can use pretty much any skin-on white fish, as long as it's really fresh. It's hearty but not heavy.

To prepare the silky tomatoes, cut the tomatoes into large chunks and blend in a blender with the olive oil until smooth. Pass through a fine sieve and set aside. Season with salt to taste.

Heat 1 tablespoon of the olive oil in a heavy-based saucepan over a medium heat. Season the fish with salt on both sides. Cook the fish skin-side down for 4 5 minutes or until the skin is crispy. Flip to the other side and cook for a further 2 minutes, or until the fish is cooked through.

Place the rest of the ingredients in a mixing bowl. Chop the pollock, with the skin on, into 2 cm (¾ in) squares and add to the bowl. Mix gently with a spoon. Put a couple of tablespoons of the silky tomatoes on a plate and pile the pollock mixture on top. Season with freshly ground black pepper.

GRILLED SQUID STUFFED
WITH SPICED LAMB SAUSAGE

Serves 4

500 g (1 lb 2 oz) whole squid
(cleaned as on page 116,
and keep the tenacles)
vegetable oil, for brushing
sea salt
Classic Tahini (page 60)
or shop-bought, to serve

**For the spiced lamb
sausage stuffing**
150 g (5½ oz) stale sourdough
200 ml (7 fl oz) milk
500 g (1 lb 2 oz) minced
(ground) lamb
15 g (½ oz) sweet paprika
12 g (½ oz) caraway seeds,
finely ground
¼ teaspoon hot chilli powder
4 garlic, crushed
50 g (1¾ oz) flat-leaf parsley
leaves, chopped
8 g (¼ oz) sea salt

I hadn't cooked this dish for a while, then my friend Roni reminded me of it when I was gathering recipes for this book, as it's one of her favourites. The squid provides a fresh contrast to the spiced lamb mix with a subtle hint of the sea. Caraway seeds have an earthy flavour that goes perfectly with the meat. This is a very interesting and rewarding way of cooking squid, and I've been preparing it like this for 20 years.

First, in a bowl, soak the sourdough in the milk for 30 minutes.

Preheat the oven to 180°C (350°F/gas 4).

Squeeze out the excess milk from the bread then add the remaining stuffing ingredients to the bowl and mix until well incorporated. Pan-fry a small quantity of the mixture to check the seasoning. If the seasoning is right, fill the squid tubes with the stuffing mixture until they are three-quarters full.

Prepare a charcoal grill or heat a griddle pan (skillet) over a high heat. If using a griddle pan, then brush it with a little olive oil.

Season the stuffed squid with a little of salt on the outside, then grill for 3–4 minutes on each side. Transfer to a baking tray, then finish cooking in the oven for 6 minutes. To serve, slice the squid and arrange on top of some tahini.

CHAPTER 10

MEAT

I've always been drawn to the more economical cuts of meat; the flavour and cooking process is much more rewarding. Ox cheek, onglet and lamb sweetbreads are perennially popular on the menu, and I love finding new ways to cook them to get the most flavour.

Lamb is more common where I come from, so a lot of my early cooking included it. Street food in Tel Aviv often uses lamb, as the terrain of the country is really suited to sheep, so they are reared in abundance.

This chapter, though, highlights the influences I've picked up from my early days in the kitchen to present day; you'll find everything from street food-inspired kebabs and grilled meats to my twist on tartare and cuts that are more commonly associated with British cooking.

LAMB AND BEEF MINCE KEBABS WITH BURNT AUBERGINE

Makes about 10

1 medium aubergine
   (eggplants)
350 g (12 oz) coarsely minced
   (ground) beef
150 g (5½ oz) coarsely minced
   (ground) lamb
2 garlic cloves, finely chopped
¾ teaspoon sea salt
½ teaspoon freshly ground
   black pepper

To serve
Classic Tahini (page 60)
   or shop-bought
Chopped Salad (page 170)
steamed basmati rice

Here I'm using a mix of lamb and beef for a more subtly flavoured kebab, allowing the other flavours that are present to shine through. The burnt aubergine (eggplant) is completely incorporated into the meat mixture – you might not even be able to see it – but the smoky flavours are there. Because the kebabs can be fragile, letting them rest in the refrigerator before cooking will help them firm up and hold together. You might be surprised by the difference the aubergine makes here – it really adds an incredible flavour.

Burn the aubergine over an open flame (either directly on the hob or on a barbecue) on all sides until the aubergine is completely scorched on the outside and soft on the inside. This process takes about 10 minutes. Transfer the aubergines to a tray to cool slightly until you can handle them (the aubergines shouldn't cool down completely as then they'll be harder to peel). Peel off the charred skin, cut off the stems and place into a sieve until most of the liquid has drained away. Then chop into large chunks.

Place the aubergine in a bowl with the minced beef and lamb, and the garlic, season with salt and pepper and mix until combined, then form cylinder-shaped kebabs (about 50–60 g/1¾–2¼ oz each). Place the kebabs on a tray and store in the refrigerator for at least 3 hours until they become firm.

Remove the kebabs from the refrigerator 20 minutes before cooking. They are best cooked over a hot charcoal grill but can also be cooked in a hot griddle pan (skillet). Cook for 4–5 minutes, turning a couple of times, until they are browned on the outside and hot through, but still pink in the middle. Serve with tahini, chopped salad and steamed basmati rice.

SLOW-ROAST LEG OF LAMB, SHAWARMA STYLE

Serves 4–6

1 tablespoon ground cumin

1 tablespoon sweet paprika

1 tablespoon turmeric

1 tablespoon ground
   coriander

1 teaspoon sea salt

1 teaspoon freshly ground
   black pepper

1 whole bone-in leg of lamb
   (2–2.5 kg/4 lb 8 oz–5 lb 8 oz)

1 whole head of garlic,
   cut in half

4 bay leaves

pitas, to serve

I think this dish will please any meat-lover. In Israel, traditional shawarma is cooked on a spit, but here we've taken the shawarma seasoning and used it as a dry rub before the meat is slowly braised until it's falling apart. This makes a great roast and is perfect to serve as a centrepiece at a family meal along with salads, sides and sauces, where everyone can dig in and assemble their own pitas.

Preheat the oven to 180°C (350°F/gas 4).

Mix all the spices and salt and pepper in a small bowl, then rub the mixture all over the lamb (using all of the spice mix). Place the lamb in a deep roasting tray (pan) with the garlic and the bay leaves and add enough water to come up to a third of the lamb leg. Cut lengths of baking parchment and aluminium foil large enough to cover the tray and seal tightly. Cook in the oven for 3–4 hours, or until the meat is falls easily off the bone. When the lamb is ready, take the tray out of the oven. As the meat will be very hot, use plastic gloves to take the meat off the bone and place on a serving platter. Keep the cooking juices and drizzle some of them on top of the meat. Serve with some pitas.

LAMB TARTARE WITH PICKLED CUCUMBERS AND AMBA

Serves 4–6

200 g (7 oz) lamb rump or
    lamb leg, trimmed of excess
    fat and tough connective
    tissue
30 g (1 oz) Pickled Cucumbers
    (page 27), finely chopped
1 small shallot, diced
1 tablespoon chives, chopped
½ teaspoon Aleppo
    chilli flakes
2 teaspoon amba
2 teaspoon extra-virgin
    olive oil
sea salt and freshly ground
    black pepper

To serve
2 toasted pitas, halved
Za'atar (page 18), for
    sprinkling

This is an unusual spin on a very classic dish: a tartare made with lamb instead of beef. The egg yolk you might usually expect to see in a tartare is missing: instead, the amba works as the binding agent, while also adding a lot of flavour. I recently started serving this with a grilled pita in the restaurant and it's had a great response. The pickled cucumber is a vital component, cutting through the rich meat and adding to the complexity of the dish.

Cut the trimmed lamb into thin strips and then into small cubes about 2.5 mm (⅟₁₆ in) in size. Place in a mixing bowl and add the rest of the ingredients. Mix well and serve with toasted pita sprinkled with za'atar.

LAMB SHANKS WITH FREEKEH

Serves 4

For the shanks

2 tablespoons vegetable oil
4 lamb shanks
sea salt and freshly ground
black pepper
2 onions, cut into large
chunks
3 carrots, peeled and cut
into large chunks
1 leek, cut into large chunks
5 celery stalks, cut into
large chunks
½ garlic head
1 tablespoon tomato
purée (paste)
4 tomatoes, chopped
(or 400 g/14 oz tin of
chopped tomatoes)
10 thyme sprigs

For the freekeh

500 g (1 lb 2 oz) freekeh
wheat, rinsed
2 garlic cloves
5 thyme sprigs
2 bay leaves
1 teaspoon sea salt
25 g (1 oz) flat-leaf parsley
leaves, finely chopped
25 g (1 oz) coriander
(cilantro), finely chopped
30 g (1 oz) spring onions
(scallions), finely chopped
25 ml (¾ fl oz) extra-virgin
olive oil
juice of 1 lemon

This is a special occasion dish to make at home, perfect for a dinner party or a special meal. Using freekeh makes it even more special. This roasted green wheat works well with anything that has juices or a sauce, as it soaks them all up while adding its own delicious, smoky flavours. Try not to overcook the freekeh. It's a very forgiving grain, unlike rice, and it won't go mushy if you do overcook it, but it is nicer with a little bite.

First, brown the lamb shanks. Heat the vegetable oil in a heavy-based saucepan over a high heat, add the lamb shanks and brown on all sides for about 8 minutes. Season generously with salt and pepper and set aside. Add the vegetables, along with the garlic head, to the pan you browned the shanks in and cook for about 10 minutes, until golden brown. Add the tomato purée to the pan and cook for a further 2 minutes, then tip in the tomatoes and return the lamb shanks to the pan. Add the thyme, season with salt and pepper, and cover with enough water to come up to about three-quarters of the lamb shanks. Cover with a lid and cook over a low heat for 2–2½ hours or until the meat is tender. If you prefer, you can cook the lamb shanks in an oven preheated to 175°C (350°F/gas 4) in a roasting tray (pan) for 3 hours – just make sure the lamb is submerged in liquid, and tightly cover the roasting tray with a double layer of aluminium foil.

To cook the freekeh, place the freekeh in a deep pot. Add the garlic cloves, thyme, bay leaves and salt. Add enough water to sit 5 cm (2 in) above the freekeh, and bring to the boil. Reduce the heat and simmer for 30 minutes, until the freekeh is tender to bite (do not overcook the freekeh as it will become starchy). When the freekeh is ready, drain it and transfer it to a bowl. Add the chopped herbs, chopped spring onions, olive oil, lemon juice, and season with salt and pepper. Serve the lamb shanks on top of the freekeh, with some of the lamb cooking liquid.

GRILLED BARNSLEY CHOP
WITH YOGHURT AND ZHOUG

Serves 2

2 Barnsley (double loin) lamb
   chops (250 g/9 oz each)
sea salt and freshly ground
   black pepper
4 tablspoons yoghurt
   (preferably thick sheep's
   yoghurt), to serve

For the zhoug

3 long green hot chillies
100 g (3½ oz) coriander
   (cilantro), coarsely chopped
2 garlic cloves, peeled
¼ teaspoon ground coriander
¼ teaspoon ground cumin
¼ teaspoon sea salt
3½ tablespoons vegetable oil

For the yoghurt
200 g (7 oz) Greek yoghurt
juice of ½ lemon

A Barnsley chop is essentially a double loin chop taken from right across the lamb's loin. It's a special cut, but your butcher should be able to provide it. You get a bit more flavour from the extra bone as it cooks, and it's one of those cuts that just feels a bit fancy. The yoghurt and zhoug make a great complement here: the tang of the yoghurt cuts through the strong flavour of the lamb, while the zhoug adds a kick and elevates the dish.

To make the zhoug, blitz all the ingredients (apart from the oil) in a food processor until you have a coarse paste. Add the vegetable oil and pulse for a couple of seconds until combined.

Whisk the yoghurt and lemon juice in a bowl until well blended. Set aside.

Prepare a charcoal grill or heat a griddle pan over a high heat.

Season the lamb chops with plenty of salt and pepper. Grill the chops over hot coals for 6 minutes, turning halfway, until medium rare. (Alternatively, preheat a cast-iron pan (skillet) to high and cook the lamb chops until medium-rare.) Set aside to rest for 5–7 minutes. Once rested, serve with yoghurt and zhoug.

GRILLED LAMB SWEETBREAD SKEWERS WITH LEMON AND ZA'ATAR

Serves 4

240 g (8½ oz) clean lamb
   (or veal) sweetbreads,
   cut into 1 cm (½ in) pieces
olive oil, for brushing
sea salt
2 tablespoons Za'atar
   (page 18)
1 tablespoon lemon juice
lemon wedges, to serve

We cook these over charcoal, which really is essential for sweetbreads as the smokiness cuts through the fat in a way you couldn't achieve by pan-frying. This is another popular dish at the restaurant: combined simply with a squeeze of lemon and our za'atar blend. It makes a great appetiser – and it pairs really well with a cold beer.

Either wooden or metal skewers can be used. If using wooden skewers, start by soaking the wooden skewers in water for a few hours before grilling, to prevent them from burning. Alternatively, use metal skewers, which don't need to be soaked.

Push the sweetbreads onto 4 skewers (60 g/2¼ oz on each skewer) and preheat a charcoal grill.

When the coals are hot and white, lightly brush the skewers with some olive oil, season with salt and place over the hot grill. Grill for 5–6 minutes, turning halfway, until the sweetbreads are thoroughly cooked and nice and golden in colour.

Remove from the grill and sprinkle generously with the za'atar and the lemon juice. Serve with lemon wedges. Eat immediately.

CHOPPED LIVER SALAD
AND PICKLED CUCUMBERS

Serves 5–6

500 g (1 lb 2 oz) chicken livers,
   cleaned and trimmed to
   remove connective tissues
3 tablespoons vegetable oil,
   for frying
700 g (1 lb 9 oz) white onions,
   finely diced
2 eggs
¾ teaspoon sea salt
⅛ teaspoon freshly ground
   black pepper

To serve

1 small Pickled Cucumber
   (page 27) per person
1 teaspoon finely chopped
   raw onion per person
Challah (page 100)

This is something my mum used to make for me at home – it's
a very traditional Ashkenazi Jewish dish that is usually eaten at
Jewish holidays. I think it's a really good way to use liver, as the
caramelised onions add a sweetness, while the pickled cucumbers
cut cleanly through the richness. If you like chicken liver paté,
you'll enjoy this.

Pat the chicken livers dry with paper towel.

Heat the oil in a frying pan (skillet) over a medium heat, add the
onions and fry for 8–10 minutes until caramelised and deep brown
in colour. Set aside.

Place the eggs in a small saucepan, cover with cold water, then
bring to the boil and boil for 8–10 minutes. Remove the eggs from
the heat and cool under cold running water. Make sure the eggs
are cooled down thoroughly otherwise you won't be able to peel
them easily.

Add more oil to the same pan over a medium heat, and when the
pan starts to smoke, add a batch of the chicken livers in a single
layer, season with salt and pepper and cook for about 4–5 minutes
on each side. Set aside to cool and repeat with the remaining
chicken livers.

Finely chop the cooled livers and hard-boiled eggs, transfer
to a bowl, add the browned onions and mix well with a spoon.
Add the salt and pepper. Taste and adjust the seasoning if needed.

Serve with chopped raw onions on top, pickled cucumber
and some challah bread.

CHARGRILLED OX HEART WITH WATERCRESS AND CHARRED RADICCHIO AND SPRING ONION

Serves 2

250 g (9 oz) ox heart, cleaned
   and cut into thin strips
50 g (1¾ oz) radicchio,
   quartered lengthwise, stem
   removed, leaves separated
6 spring onions (scallions),
   trimmed to 6 cm (2½ in)
   of the white part and
   some of the green
50 g (1¾ oz) watercress
1 tablespoon olive oil
1 tablespoon lemon juice
sea salt and freshly ground
   black pepper

For the marinade
25 ml (¾ fl oz) olive oil
4 garlic cloves, crushed
5 oregano, sage
   or rosemary sprigs

You might have to place a special order with your butcher for ox heart, but it's worth it to make this. This is a good offal dish for beginners, as ox heart is quite a lean meat and doesn't have the same iron-heavy flavour you might get with duck or chicken hearts. When treated correctly – thinly sliced and cooked over a charcoal grill – it tastes almost like strips of steak. The simple garlic and herb marinade complements it perfectly, and it pairs so well with the warm salad of grilled radicchio, which is cut through with lemon for another layer of flavour.

Combine the strips of ox heart with the marinade ingredients in a bowl. Cover and leave to marinate in the refrigerator for 24 hours.

When ready to cook, preheat a charcoal grill and remove the meat from the marinade.

Start by grilling the radicchio leaves on both sides (without oil) for 3–4 minutes, until tender. Repeat with the spring onions and set them aside. Grill the strips of marinated meat for 1–2 minutes on each side, no longer.

Combine the grilled vegetables, watercress and heart in a bowl, drizzle with the olive oil and lemon juice and season with salt and pepper.

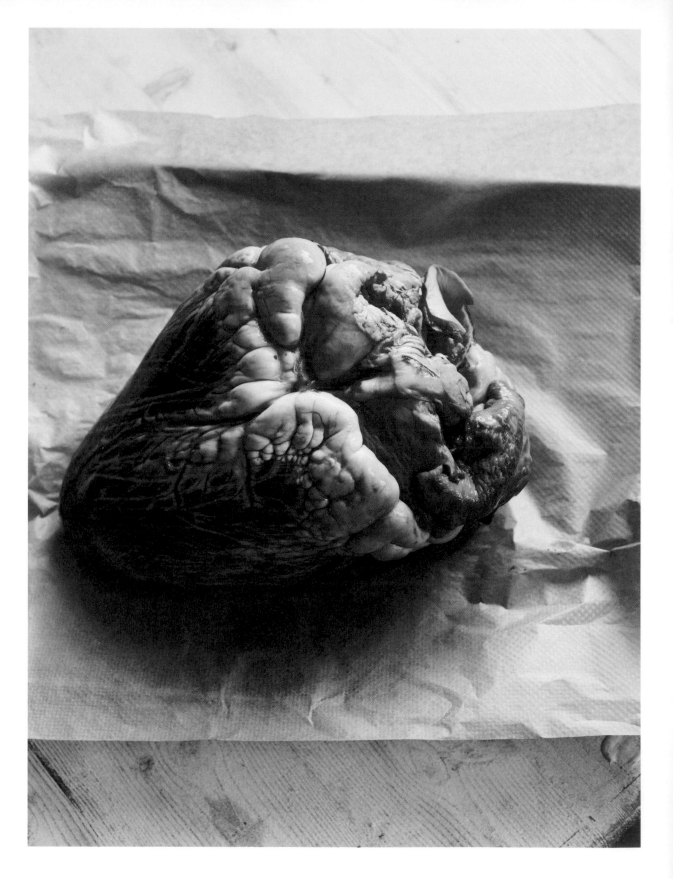

OREN

BEEF CHEEKS AND HUMMUS

Serves 4

vegetable oil, for cooking
1.5 kg (3 lb 5 oz) trimmed
    beef cheeks
sea salt and freshly ground
    black pepper
100 g (3½ oz) onions,
    cut into 2 cm (3¼ in) cubes
250 g (9 oz) leeks
2 carrots, peeled and
    cut into 2 cm (3¼ in) cubes
45 g (1½ oz) tomato
    purée (paste)
200 ml (7 fl oz/scant 1 cup)
    dry red wine
5 bay leaves
½ garlic head
600 ml (20 fl oz/2½ cups)
    good-quality beef stock,
    plus optional extra 300 ml
    (10 fl oz/1¼ cups) to reheat
    the cheeks
2 tablespoons Hummus
    (page 63) per person,
    to serve

This dish is such a crowd pleaser. Beef cheek has a lot of unique qualities; it's lean, but there's a layer of fat within the meat that melts when you cook it, which makes it extra flavourful and special. Hummus is sometimes served with ground lamb or beef in Israel, so I took inspiration from that, but when I put the beef cheeks and hummus together, it became something else entirely. Hummus was the accompaniment, not the other way around. It is very simple even though it takes a little time, and it's very rewarding, as the meat becomes extremely tender and delicious.

Heat a large, heavy-based ovenproof dish with a drizzle of oil over a high heat. Season the meat generously with salt and pepper on all sides. When the pan starts to smoke, add the meat in batches (do not overcrowd the pan as the cheeks won't seal properly) and brown on all sides. Remove the meat from the pan and set aside.

Add a drizzle more oil, then add the vegetables to the pan and cook until over a medium heat until caramelised at the edges – this can take 20–25 minutes, so be patient.

Preheat the oven to 160°C (320°F/gas 3).

Add the tomato purée and red wine to the vegetables in the pan and cook until the wine has reduced by half. Return the beef cheeks to the pan, add the bay leaves, garlic and cover with stock. Bring to the boil and cover tightly with foil and cook in the oven for 2½–3 hours. The best way to check the meat is done is to take one cheek out onto a plate and to taste it – it should be really soft, but not falling apart.

Gently remove the meat from the pan and keep covered in a warm place. Pass the stock through a fine sieve into a small saucepan and set over medium heat. Reduce the stock by simmering it for a few minutes until reduced by two-thirds. Strain and serve the cheeks with the sauce and hummus.

SPICED DUCK-HEART SKEWERS WITH BAHĀRĀT AND SOUR CREAM

Serves 4

16 duck hearts, cleaned
of excess fat and blood
4 tablespoons thick sour
cream
sea salt

For the bahārāt spice blend
½ teaspoon ground cinnamon
¼ teaspoon ground green
cardamom seeds
¼ teaspoon ground cloves
½ teaspoon ground aniseed
½ teaspoon ground cumin
¼ teaspoon ground black
pepper
¼ teaspoon sweet paprika

I love duck heart – the flavour is slightly gamier than that of a chicken, and it has a little more fat, too. The bahārāt spice blend works perfectly because the meat can hold up to the strong, aromatic flavour. When dipped in sour cream, everything melds together into something a little more mellow, but still very impactful. It's really popular at the restaurant, and I personally love to serve it as an starter (appetiser) or snack.

Prepare a charcoal grill.

To make the bahārāt spice blend, mix all the spices together.

Either wooden or metal skewers can be used. If using wooden skewers, start by soaking the wooden skewers in water for a few hours before grilling, to prevent them from burning. Alternatively, use metal skewers, which don't need to be soaked.

Divide the cleaned hearts among 4 skewers (4 on each skewer) and season generously with the bahārāt mix, and salt.

Grill the skewers on both sides for 3–4 minutes – you want the hearts to still be pink in the middle. Serve with sour cream.

ABOUT THE AUTHOR

Oded Oren has worked in a number of the Tel Aviv's feted restaurants, such as the famed Turkiz and Food Art, Tamuz. He has also undertaken a series of stages in some of the world's best kitchens, which resulted in his permanent move to London, via California and Paris. In 2011, he founded a catering business and then in 2019, he opened his restaurant, Oren. This is his first book.

ACKNOWLEDGEMENTS

Firstly, to Roni Belfer; thanks for the support and for reminding me of some really special recipes of mine that I had forgotten!

To Lisa De Blauw and Sam Lone from Oren, and Hanne and Jo for opening a door, and for your friendship.

Thank you to Valerie Berry, Issy Croker and Tabitha Hawkins, and to Benjamin McMahon for the continued support.

To Itiel Zion, Sahul Tevet, Jasmino, Me & Me, Hanan Margilan, M25, and Tali Knipe for being such a good pal. Tal Oron, Yotam Laufer, Eilon Bregman, Eyal Baumert, Studio ETC, Benjamin Chapman, Turkiz and Feya Buchvlad – thanks for pushing me and being a good friend all the years. Also thanks to Douglas Lavin, Nud Dudhia, Claire Ptak, Julie and Michael Seelig, Efi Segal, Harry Livesey, George Fredenham and Yosi Romano.

Finally, thank you to Eve Marleau and Eila Purvis for all your help in the making of this book.

INDEX

Published in 2022 by Hardie Grant Books,
an imprint of Hardie Grant Publishing

Hardie Grant Books (London)
5th & 6th Floors
52–54 Southwark Street
London SE1 1UN

Hardie Grant Books (Melbourne)
Building 1, 658 Church Street
Richmond, Victoria 3121

hardiegrantbooks.com

Text © Oded Oren
Photography © Issy Croker
Photography on pages 9, 10–11, 21, 22, 23, 42, 43, 50–51, 62, 66, 67, 69, 81–82,
110, 112, 113, 120–121, 127, 128, 135, 138–139, 152–153, 158, 159, 166, 167, 175, 178,
180–181, 200, 210, 217, 224, 228–229 © Itiel Zion
Photography on pages 96, 240, 242–243, 245, 247, 248–249 © Benjamin
McMahon
Image on page 4 © Oded Oren

British Library Cataloguing-in-Publication Data. A catalogue
record for this book is available from the British Library.

Oren
ISBN: 9781-78488-443-7

10 9 8 7 6 5 4 3 2 1

Publishing Director: Kajal Mistry
Acting Publishing Director: Emma Hopkin
Commissioning Editor: Eve Marleau
Editor: Eila Purvis
Design and Art Direction: Stuart Hardie
Photographer: Issy Croker
Photography Assistants: India Whiley-Morton and Elliyah Cleveley
Food Stylist: Valerie Berry
Food Stylist Assistant: Hanna Miller
Prop Stylist: Tabitha Hawkins
Copy-editor: Laura Nickoll
Proofreader: Kate Wanwimolruk
Indexer: Cathy Heath
Production Controller: Sabeena Atchia

Colour reproduction by p2d
Printed and bound in China by Leo Paper Products Ltd.

MIX
Paper from
responsible sources
FSC™ C020056
FSC
www.fsc.org